WICKED WORLD CUP

Other titles in The Knowledge series:

Flaming Olympics
by Michael Coleman

Potty Politics
by Terry Deary

Foul Football
by Michael Coleman

Murderous Maths
by Kjartan Poskitt

The Gobsmacking Galaxy
by Kjartan Poskitt

Awful Art
by Michael Cox

Mind-blowing Music
by Michael Cox

Groovy Movies
by Martin Oliver

WICKED WORLD CUP

MICHAEL COLEMAN

Illustrated by
Harry Venning

Hippo

For Matthew, my favourite wicked full-back!

Scholastic Children's Books,
Commonwealth House, 1–19 New Oxford Street,
London WC1A 1NU, UK
A division of Scholastic Limited
London ~ New York ~ Toronto ~ Sydney ~ Auckland

Published in the UK by Scholastic Ltd, 1998
Text copyright © Michael Coleman, 1998
Illustrations copyright © Harry Venning, 1998
Cover illustration copyright © Philip Reeve, 1998

ISBN 0 590 19713 4

Typeset by TW Typesetting, Midsomer Norton, Somerset
Printed by Cox & Wyman Ltd, Reading, Berks.

10 9 8 7 6 5 4 3 2 1

The right of Michael Coleman and Harry Venning to be identified
as the author and illustrator of this work respectively has been
asserted by them in accordance with the Copyright, Designs and
Patents Act, 1988.

Contents

Introduction 7
Wicked World Cup beginnings 9

1930: Unbeatable Uruguay 23
Getting a-head in the world! 25

1934: Invincible Italy 29
Wicked wonders: Vittorio Pozzo and
inconsistent Italy 31

1938: Italy 'it 'em again 35
Qualifying quandaries 39

1950: Uruguay surprise 45
The management game 48

1954: Germany grab it 54
Wicked Wonders: Ferenc Puskas and
the magical Magyars 58

1958: Brilliant Brazil 64
Wicked Wonders: Pelé and the brilliant
Brazilians 65

1962: Brilliant Brazil – again 74
Medicine men 76

1966: Alf's England 'eroes 81
Serious superstitions 88

1970: Brazil go nuts 91
Wicked wonders: The two Bobby's of England 93

1974: German genius 99
Wicked wonders: "Kaiser Franz" and Germany 101

1978: Argentine argy-bargy 105
The terrible telly, wicked words
and naughty newspapers 108

1982: Italian inspiration 116
Wicked celebrations 118

1986: Argentina get a big hand 120
Wicked wonders: Diego Maradona and Argentina 124

1990: German jubillation 135
Wicked fans 138

1994: Brazil's braves 142
Kool kit 146

1998: Ooh-ah, who'll go far? 149

Results – fill-it-in chart 155

INTRODUCTION

Here's a wicked question to try on your football-mad friends:

- in Brazil it's known as the *Campeonato Mundial de Futebol*
- in Germany it's called the *Fussball-Weltmeisterschaft*
- in France it's the *Coupe du Monde*
- in Spain it's the *Copa del Mundo de Futbol*

What is it?

The answer, of course, is the football World Cup – the "FIFA World Cup" to give it its proper title. It's the biggest, the best, and the most wicked football tournament there is!

It's the *biggest* because, although the finals are only held every four years, the whole competition takes well over two years to complete.

It's the *best* because it's a competition to find the best football nation in the world.

And it's the *most wicked* because, in its history, the World Cup has seen a whole collection of...

- wicked matches, like the rough one in 1954 that was continued in the changing rooms after the final whistle had blown!
- wicked teams, like the one that was nicknamed "the Mickey Mouse and Donald Duck team"!

- wicked players, like the one who was sent off in 1966 but refused to go!
- wicked fans, like the Mexican horn-honkers!
- wicked referees, like the one who was a real monster!

Yes, you'll find them all in this book together with loads of wicked facts and wicked quotes, not to mention plenty of wicked questions you can use to fool your know-all friends, teachers, Dads (and Mums).

So read on to find out everything you need to know about the World Cup.

It's wicked!

WICKED WORLD CUP – BEGINNINGS!

So you're a fan of international football? Here's a question you should be able to answer, then! What were the opening words of the hit pop song *Three Lions* which became the England team's theme song in the 1996 European Championships?

Why? Because the game of Association Football certainly *began* in England. The first rules for the game were developed at Cambridge University in 1848 and the oldest existing football club in the world is Sheffield FC, which was formed in 1857.

Although football may have started in England, however, it quickly spread to the other parts of the world – to Scotland, Wales and Northern Ireland for a start!

In their wicked pasts the four countries of Great Britain had enjoyed knocking lumps out of each other on the battlefield. So, as football grew in popularity, it was only natural that they would want to start doing the same thing on the football field. Because these matches were between national teams they were called "internationals" – and some of them were really wicked!

Here's your timeline for how things went.

1872 The first ever official international football match takes place – at a cricket ground! This was the West of Scotland Cricket Ground, in Partick. Scotland and England drew 0–0. It cost 5p to get in! The closest the crowd of 2000 comes to seeing a goal is when a shot by Leckie of Scotland lands on top of the tape stretched between the posts; crossbars haven't been invented yet!

1873 England and Scotland play the second-ever international (again at a cricket ground – the famous Oval, in London) and the first-ever international goal is scored as England win 4–2. After this, the match becomes an annual fixture.

1876 Wales play their first international match, against Scotland. They don't start off too well, losing 0–4!

1880 The Irish play their first international match, against England. They do even worse, losing 0–13!

10

1884 England, Northern Ireland, Scotland and Wales start the "Home International" Championship. The four countries play each other during the season in a league competition, with 2 points for a win and 1 point for a draw. The first champions are Scotland, who win all three of their matches.

1888 The first "World Cup" match – except that it's played between two club sides! Renton, the Scottish FA Cup winners, beat the English FA Cup winners, West Bromwich Albion, to win a match billed as "The Football Championship of the World"!

1895 Ace goalscorer Steve Bloomer scores twice on his debut for England in the 9–0 victory over Northern Ireland. The age of the international star player has arrived ...

Bloomin' brilliant!

Don't be fooled by his name – Steve Bloomer wasn't a player who made mistakes! Born in 1874, he was England's star striker, the Alan Shearer of the early years of international football. He didn't look like a footballer, though. In fact he was so weedy his team-mates called him "Paleface", but in 23 games for England he scored 28 goals, hitting the target in each of his first 10 internationals!

● One of his finest games was against Wales, in 1896. Bloomer scored 5 goals. Afterwards a news-paper report described him as being: "as slippery as an eel".

● He liked the ball at his feet, from where he could shoot on sight. If it didn't happen he was known to shout at team-mates: "What d'ye call that? A pass? I haven't got an aeroplane!" If it did happen, it seems that Steve Bloomer usually scored, because his goalscoring record for his clubs was as fantastic as his international record. Between 1892 and 1914, playing for Derby County (twice) and Middlesbrough, he hit 353 goals in 598 league matches.

● Nowadays, star players earn a lot of money. Not only do they get paid a lot, they can also earn a fortune out of deals with sportswear manufacturers. Times have changed. When Steve Bloomer signed for Derby County in 1891 he was paid 37½p a week! Mind you, he was one of the first footballers to be associated with sporting goods. A boot and shoe company brought out a new range of football boots and called them "Bloomer's Lucky Strikers"!

● Steve Bloomer retired at the age of 40, but still stayed involved with football. He went to coach in Germany.

There have many international superstars since then, but not too many of them have had a monument erected in their honour. Steve Bloomer has. It's in the centre of Derby and was put up in 1997. Part of the money was raised by selling the player's international caps.

Marvellous Meredith!

Billy Meredith, born in the same year as Steve Bloomer, was the other big international star at the turn of the century. Meredith was a wicked winger – in more ways than one. He was banned from playing for a year in 1905 after being found guilty of offering the Aston Villa captain £10 to lose a game and help his club, Manchester City, win the league!

In spite of this, Meredith is rightly remembered for his footballing ability. Unlike Steve Bloomer, the mustachioed Meredith did look like a footballer. He was as lean as a greyhound and ran like one. The sight of him racing up and down the touchline, with his trademark toothpick clamped between his teeth, always brought the crowd to its feet – which is why he earned the nickname: "The Prince of Wingers".

Meredith was incredibly fit. Over a period of 25 years, he won 48 caps for Wales. His last game, in 1920, when he was 45 years and 8 months old, must have been the best of the lot. It was against England at Arsenal's ground, Highbury, and Wales won 2–1 – the first time they'd ever beaten England!

That may have been his last international, but Billy Meredith played on for another four years after that, turning out for Manchester City in the 1924 FA Cup semi-final when he was four months short of his 50th birthday.

Football followers!

Fool your football-fanatic teacher with this wicked trick question! How far apart are the Everton and Liverpool grounds?

Answer: at least 700 miles (1200 km)!

Then, when he or she says: "What a lemon you are! Any fool knows that Liverpool and Everton both play in the City of Liverpool and their grounds aren't more than a mile apart", you quickly point out that you weren't talking about the *English* teams Liverpool and Everton. You were talking about the Liverpool who play in Uruguay and the Everton who play in Chile!

How did they get these names? Because, even though the English, Irish, Scots and Welsh might have thought so at the time, football wasn't only being played in the British Isles in the 19th century. It was being spread worldwide by all sorts of people who had gone overseas to work: sailors, soldiers, merchants, engineers – even teachers and pupils! For instance:

- The Argentinian club, Buenos Aires, was formed by British residents in 1865 … only eight years after Sheffield FC in England.
- The first international outside the UK took place in

South America, when Uruguay played Argentina in 1901.

Most often the people who introduced the game to a country were British or Italian. That's how some overseas football clubs ended up with team names we know in Britain – the people who spread the game named them after their favourite club back home.

Train-ing, Brazilian-style!

Brazil, the country destined to be the first to win the World Cup three times, might never have discovered football if it hadn't been for an Englishman. In the early 1880s a man named Charles Miller, whose parents had emigrated to Brazil, was sent to England to study. He stayed away for ten years. When he finally returned he was carrying:

● some academic qualifications

● two footballs

● a complete set of football kit!

Miller had discovered football while he had been in England and had played for Southampton. Back in Brazil he enthusiastically set about convincing everybody what a great game football was. British workers who had been sent to Brazil such as those of the São Paulo Railway were the first to start playing. They took part in the first recognized football match in Brazil, beating a team from the Gas Company 4–2. Obviously down to the Rail team's superior *train*ing!

Russians get the boot

Two Englishmen, the Charnock brothers, took the game to Russia in 1887. They owned a mill near Moscow, a fact which proved to be very handy. The brothers had managed to get everything they needed to start a football team – except for football boots. The problem was solved by getting a leather worker at the mill to nail studs to the worker's shoes!

It worked, too. By 1900 the Moscow League had started and the Charnocks' team won it the first five years running.

Germany

English schoolboys living in Germany are supposed to have played football in the 1860s and so introduced the game to the country. In 1899 the first ever foreign football tour was made by England to Germany to help spread the game.

So whenever England get beaten by Germany they've only got themselves to blame!

Olympic champions

At the turn of the century, *the* world sporting festival was the Olympic Games. From 1896 it has been staged every four years, missing out only during the First and Second World Wars. To be an Olympic champion meant that you were a world champion.

> ## Wicked World Cup question
> Football made its first appearance in the Olympics, as a demonstration sport, in the 1900 Games in Paris. Did the first Olympic football champions come from the East, or from the West?
> **Wicked answer:** From the East – the East End of London! A club side, Upton Park FC, represented Great Britain. They only had to play one game and became "world champions" by beating France 4–0!

Champion England

Football entered the Olympics as an accepted sport in 1908, when the Games were staged in London. This time it was a proper tournament and a proper Great Britain team entered (not just England). What's more they won, beating Denmark 2–0 in the final. Just to prove it wasn't a fluke, they did it again four years later when the 1912 Olympics took place in Sweden. Once more they met Denmark in the final, this time winning 4–2 to take the gold medal. (And it was *the* gold medal. Team members didn't get one each in the early days of the Olympics, they had to share.)

After that, the record wasn't so good.

1920 Did not enter. The 1914–18 World War had just ended and the British weren't prepared to play football against rotten foreigners who'd spent four years trying to blow their heads off!

1924 Did not enter again, same reason as 1920.

1928 Did not enter, this time as a protest. What about? Money. The Olympics were supposed to be for amateurs – that is, for people who weren't paid for taking part in their sport – and the British took this very seriously. When the Olympics organizers agreed to allow players to be given money, called "broken-time" payments, to make up for the wages they'd lose by taking part in the Games, the British resigned.

By not taking part, the British missed what would have been a real challenge. In 1924 the first South American country, Uruguay, had taken part – and won the gold medal! Displaying the sort of ball skills the Europeans had never seen, they scored 20 goals in five games, letting in only two.

Four years later, in 1928, Uruguay did it again. What's more, the other finalists also came from South America – Argentina.

So, football was now a world game. Uruguay's victories had shown that the South American countries had not only caught up with the Europeans but overtaken them! Or had they? Were Uruguay *really* the best team in the world?

Doubts existed because of the Olympic's rule about only allowing amateurs to take part. By 1928 many of the best players in the world were professionals. So how, it was argued, could the Olympic competition really find the best team in the world if many of the countries had been handicapped by having to leave half their players at home? It couldn't.

And, as the Olympic rules weren't going to be changed, the only other possibility was to hold a competition in which professional footballers *could* play.

What the game needed was its own World Cup. But who would organize it? Enter FIFA. At last...

FIFA and the World Cup

FIFA, which stands for *Fédération Internationale de Football Association* (in English, the "International Federation of Football Associations") had been set up in 1904 by a number of European countries who had set up club competitions and established their own Football Associations. FIFA had 7 founder members...

Odd Countries Out

Which of these countries *were* founder members of FIFA?

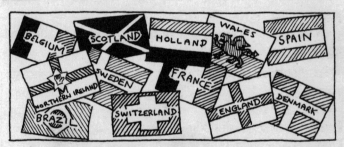

mainly because they weren't invited to join.
were no non-European countries involved either –
founder members. They all joined in 1905. There
members. None of the home countries were
Spain, Switzerland and Sweden were the founder
Answers: Belgium, Denmark, France, Holland,

Bagsy we run the World Cup, so there!

One of the things that FIFA did in 1904 was to say that it was the only group allowed to organize a professional World Cup football competition. Having said it, they did nothing about it until 1928!

Then, as the Olympics grumbling grew, they acted. Led by two Frenchmen, Jules Rimet and Henri Delauney, FIFA finally got around to using the right they'd voted themselves in 1904. The World Cup was born, and the first tournament scheduled for 1930.

Any country who was a member of FIFA could take part. Unfortunately this didn't include England, Northern Ireland, Scotland and Wales. They had all resigned from FIFA after the row about broken-time payments for taking part in the Olympics – and they hadn't got around to joining again.

Which meant that they missed the boat to the first ever World Cup finals...

1930 UNBEATABLE URUGUAY

Host Country
URUGUAY

Winners
URUGUAY

Runners Up
ARGENTINA

No. of Teams Entered **13**

Third Place
UNITED STATES

No. of Teams in Finals **13**

Fourth Place
YUGOSLAVIA

Goals Scored
70 IN 80 GAMES

Top Scorer
GUILLERMO STABILE (Argentina) – **8 IN 4 GAMES**

The first-ever World Cup competition took place in South America, in Uruguay. Why was a country so far away from Europe chosen? (Remember, it took three weeks to get from Europe to South America in those days.) There were two reasons:

- Uruguay were the reigning Olympic champions, which made them the "unofficial" world champions at the time. Having the first tournament held in their country seemed only fair.
- 1930 was also a special year for Uruguay, being the 100th year of their independence from Brazil.

So, Uruguay it was!

Unfortunately a lot of other countries felt the same way. Only 13 countries entered, which meant that the original plan for a knockout competition had to be scrapped. Instead the teams were arranged into 4 league groups (1 x 4, 3 x 3), with the winners of each group going into the semi-final.

One of these four teams was the United States of America. Five out of the eleven players in the team had been professional footballers in Scotland who'd emigrated. Maybe they should have been called the United Scots of America! They were certainly well-built players, because the other teams nicknamed them "The Shot-Putters"!

I call this game 'Tossing the Defender'

The first ever final was between old enemies Uruguay (whose solid defence had its own nickname:

"The Iron Curtain") and Argentina. After being beaten by the Uruguayans in the 1928 Olympic final, the Argentinian fans were looking for revenge. Forget cries like Eng-land! Eng-land! Their chant was:

ARGENTINA, YES! URUGUAY NO! VICTORY OR DEATH!

Not surprisingly, they were all searched for guns before they were allowed into the ground!

The referee insisted on a guard for himself and his linesmen before he'd agree to begin the match. Throughout the game, soldiers with fixed bayonets patrolled the ground.

Even so, the referee still had to solve a problem before a ball was kicked. That was the problem – which ball? Each team had brought their own ball, and wanted the game to be played with it. In the end, they agreed to play one half of the match with each ball. Argentina won the toss and were 2–1 ahead by half-time with their ball.

They then switched to Uruguay's ball for the second half – and Uruguay banged it into the net three times to win 4–2 and become the first World Cup champions!

Getting "A-head" in the world!

All footballers who play in the World Cup have reached the top of the game. But here are some who got "a-head" in different ways!

25

- Pedro Petrone played in Uruguay's 1930 winning team ... in spite of the fact that he refused ever to head the ball because it spoiled his hairstyle!

- Tostao, an important member of Brazil's 1970 team, wouldn't head the ball either. In his case it was on doctor's orders. He had an eye condition and heading the ball could have made him go blind.

- Rajko Mitic, playing for Yugoslavia in the 1950 finals, had a big head. Leaving the dressing room before the match against Brazil he whacked it against an iron beam. The game had to start without him. By the time he finally appeared, with his head swathed in bandages, Yugoslavia had already let in a goal and were on their way to a 0–2 defeat.

- Borislav Mikhailov, Bulgaria's 1994 goalkeeper, didn't only guard his goal. He guarded his hair as well. He'd recently had it transplanted at a cost of $30,000! Mikhailov was so concerned about it that he flew his hairdresser to the tournament to help him look after it. As Bulgaria fought their way to the semi-finals, Mikhailov's new hair was seen so often on TV it became world famous. When he got back home to Bulgaria he cashed in on it by opening – yes, a hair salon!

Name games!

One of the great things about the World Cup is coming across a whole batch of wicked names from around the world.

Some of them aren't real – like the time the wickedly tricky England winger Stanley Matthews was listed in a Swiss match programme as "St. Matthews"!

But some of them are – like the Cameroon striker whose name might well pop up in 1998: Jean-Jacques Misse-Misse!

Here's a whole squad-full of names from World Cup history:

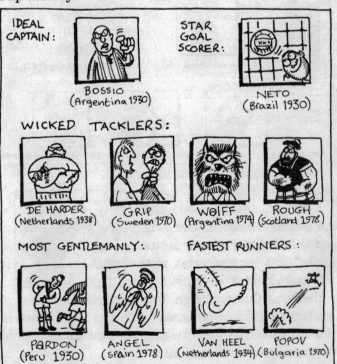

IDEAL CAPTAIN:
BOSSIO
(Argentina 1930)

STAR GOAL SCORER:
NETO
(Brazil 1930)

WICKED TACKLERS:

DE HARDER
(Netherlands 1938)

GRIP
(Sweden 1970)

WOIFF
(Argentina 1974)

ROUGH
(Scotland 1978)

MOST GENTLEMANLY:

PARDON
(Peru 1930)

ANGEL
(Spain 1978)

FASTEST RUNNERS:

VAN HEEL
(Netherlands 1934)

POPOV
(Bulgaria 1970)

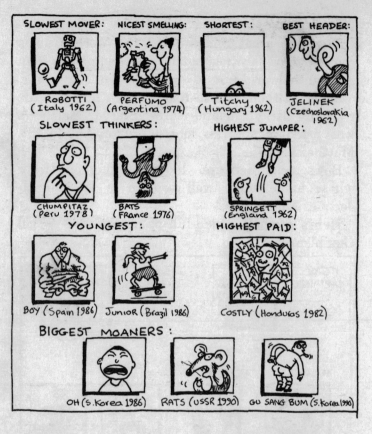

SLOWEST MOVER: ROBOTTI (Italy 1962)

NICEST SMELLING: PERFUMO (Argentina 1974)

SHORTEST: Titchy (Hungary 1962)

BEST HEADER: JELINEK (Czechoslovakia 1962)

SLOWEST THINKERS: CHUMPITAZ (Peru 1978), BATS (France 1976)

HIGHEST JUMPER: SPRINGETT (England 1962)

YOUNGEST: BOY (Spain 1986), JUNIOR (Brazil 1986)

HIGHEST PAID: COSTLY (Honduras 1982)

BIGGEST MOANERS: OH (S.Korea 1986), RATS (USSR 1990), GU SANG BUM (S.Korea 1990)

Finally, there was the Austrian referee whose real name left every player in no doubt that he was a bit of a monster: Herr Frankenstein!

Sadly, although Herr Frankenstein refereed a qualifying match, he wasn't selected to officiate in the final tournament (which he probably thought was a monstrous decision).

1934 INVINCIBLE ITALY

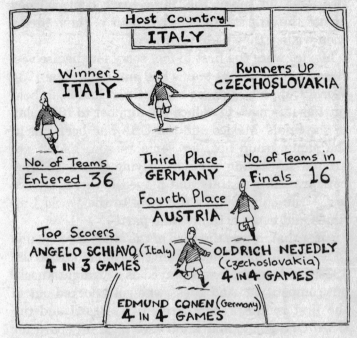

Host Country
ITALY

Winners
ITALY

Runners Up
CZECHOSLOVAKIA

No. of Teams Entered **36**

Third Place
GERMANY

Fourth Place
AUSTRIA

No. of Teams in Finals **16**

Top Scorers
ANGELO SCHIAVO (Italy)
4 IN 3 GAMES

OLDRICH NEJEDLY (Czechoslovakia)
4 IN 4 GAMES

EDMUND CONEN (Germany)
4 IN 4 GAMES

Uruguay umbrage

Some teams were selected but decided not to appear. The most important of these was Uruguay, the reigning champions. Still peeved that so few European countries had made the journey to South America in 1930, they decided to get their own back and refused to travel to Europe. They're the only champions in the history of the World Cup not to defend their title.

(In case you're wondering, England, Northern Ireland, Scotland and Wales still hadn't rejoined FIFA, so they didn't take part either.).

29

Was it worth the trip?

Four teams – the USA, Mexico, Argentina and Brazil – did make the three-week boat journey across the Atlantic to Italy. All four of them pretty soon wished they hadn't bothered.

Mexico were the first to feel sorry for themselves. Because a total of 31 teams had entered for the 1934 World Cup, a qualifying competition had been held (just as it is now) to reduce the number to 16 to play in the finals. Mexico and the USA had been put in the same group but, for some reason, hadn't got around to playing their qualifying game. So they both travelled to Italy and played it there! Mexico lost – the only country to travel to the World Cup finals and never actually take part!

After that, it was the turn of the other three teams to feel miserable. There wasn't a league part to the 1934 tournament, it was played as a straight knock-out competition. And guess who got knocked out in the first round proper? Argentina, Brazil and the USA! One game, and they were back on board for another three-week voyage home.

30

Orsi, Orsi, don't you stop

In the final, the home country Italy played Czechoslovakia. It was a game famous for a spectacular goal. With ten minutes to go and Italy losing 0–1, the Italians' left-winger Raimondo Orsi got the ball. Racing through, he pretended to shoot with his left foot – then suddenly switched and whacked it with his right foot instead. The move completely fooled the goalkeeper and the ball flew into the net.

Wicked World Cup fact

The day after the final, Orsi tried to do his trick again for the newspaper photographers. He couldn't manage it, even without a goalkeeper in the goal. He tried 20 times then gave up!

The game then went into extra time, for Italy to win with another odd goal. One of Italy's forwards, Meazza, had been injured and was limping on the right wing. (No substitutes in those days, remember.) Because of this, the Czechoslovakians didn't have anybody marking him. So when he got the ball, Meazza had plenty of time to centre it for somebody else to hit the winner!

Wicked wonders: Vittorio Pozzo and inconsistent Italy

Italy are one of the most successful World Cup nations, having won the competition three times – in 1934, 1938 and 1982 – and been runners-up twice.

One of the biggest figures in Italian football history isn't a player, but a coach. His name was Vittorio Pozzo (pronounced "Pots-o") – and he was a Manchester United supporter! Vittorio was sent to study in England by his parents, and there he discovered football. Manchester United were his favourite team and they convinced him that football was the best sport in the world. You could say that Pozzo was potty about the game!

In fact, when the time came to go home to Italy he didn't want to leave. In the end his family had to buy his ticket for him.

Once in Italy, though, he set about coaching the game he loved and became one of the longest-serving and successful coaches ever. Starting in 1912 with the Italian team which played in the Olympic Games, he was his country's coach for over 25 years, being in charge of the side until after the 1938 World Cup.

In fact, with Vittorio Pozzo as coach during the 1930s, Italy became almost invincible. In 10 years they lost only 7 games! As well as winning the World Cup in both 1934 and 1938, the team won the 1936 Olympic football gold medal too.

From then on, Italy have either done very well or
very badly in World Cups.

During the 1950s, a lot of this was because they
were recovering from a terrible disaster. In 1949 a
plane carrying the top Italian club team Torino had
crashed and the whole team had been killed. Ten of
them were Italian internationals. In 1966, however,
they just played badly! Up against tiny North
Korea, the highly-paid Italian stars lost 0–1. When
the team went home, fans waited at the airport to
pelt them with rubbish!

Sometimes it's been thought that Italians take the
game rather too seriously. In 1974 Italian players
were accused by their Polish opponents of offering
them money to lose a World Cup match that Italy
had to win to stay in the competition. Amazingly,
the Poles claimed that the attempted bribery took

place *during* the game! True or not, it didn't work: Poland won 2–1 and Italy were knocked out.

Despite this, Italy's record in international and World Cup matches is impressive! Their 3–0 qualifying round win against Moldova in 1996 included the 1000th goal scored by the team in international matches. It was scored by Christian Vieri – who was playing his first game for Italy!

Wicked World Cup fact

Italians have their own word for football – but, unlike virtually every other language, the word doesn't come from the Italian words for "foot" and "ball". They call the game *calcio* – which is actually the name of a 27-a-side game which was popular in the 16th century.

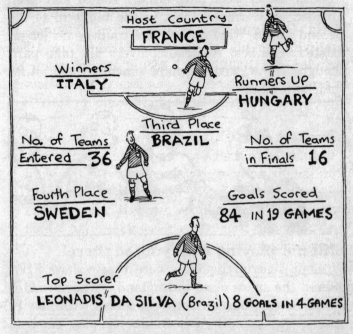

1938: ITALY 'IT 'EM AGAIN

Host Country
FRANCE

Winners
ITALY

Runners Up
HUNGARY

Third Place
BRAZIL

No. of Teams Entered 36

No. of Teams in Finals 16

Fourth Place
SWEDEN

Goals Scored
84 IN 19 GAMES

Top Scorer
LEONADIS DA SILVA (Brazil) 8 GOALS IN 4 GAMES

The competition in 1938 saw some pretty wicked stuff taking place before a ball had been kicked!

Sulking

Argentina had wanted to host the finals, arguing that the competition should have moved back to South America after being held in Europe in 1934. They lost the argument and refused to take part. So did Uruguay, who were still sulking from 1930!

Fighting

Spain didn't take part because they were fighting each other in a civil war.

Not fighting

Austria didn't take part either. They'd just been invaded by Germany (part of the build-up to the Second World War) and so the country no longer existed. The best Austrian players did take part, though. The wicked Germans pinched them all for their own team!

Still not playing with you, so there!

Without Austria, the finals were a team short. FIFA offered the spare place to England – who turned it down! So the tournament went ahead with just 15 teams. Sweden, who'd been due to play Austria, received a bye to become the only team ever to reach the quarter-finals of the competition without playing a match!

Leonidas, the brilliant Brazilian

The undoubted star of the tournament was the Brazilian striker, Leonidas da Silva. He finished top scorer with 8 goals. Four of them came in the Brazilians' first-round match against Poland.

In very muddy conditions, Leonidas scored a first-half hat-

trick to put Brazil 3–1 ahead. He wasn't satisfied
with his performance, though, and thought if he
made one change he'd play even better. So when he
trotted out for the second half ... he wasn't wearing
any boots! Much to his disgust, the referee made
him put them back on again. With Leonidas in a bad
mood, Poland pulled back to 4–4 by full-time. The
Brazilian star then decided to stop worrying about
his boots and pull his socks up instead. He scored
again, to help Brazil finally win an amazing match
6–5!

Brazil the Bruisers

Brazil beat Czechoslovakia in the next round, but
this time in a wicked way. They had more of their
players sent off! In one of the dirtiest World Cup
games ever, two Brazilians and one Czech were sent
off. On top of that, one Czech was carried off with a
broken leg and another with a bad stomach injury.

The score in goals? 1–1. Brazil went on to win the
replay 2–1 in a really quiet game.

Brazil the Brash

In their semi-final, Brazil met Italy. They were so
confident of beating them that they made eight
changes to their team, leaving out Leonidas and

some other players to rest them for the final!

It was a disastrous decision. After being 0–0 at half-time Italy scored, then won a penalty. Up stepped the Italian captain, Meazza, who'd been playing for a while in a pair of ripped shorts. In went the penalty – and down came his shorts! It didn't matter. Italy were through to the final, and Brazil were down and out (like Meazza's shorts).

Italy in time

Brazil's overconfidence even affected Italy's chances in the final. The match was being held in Paris and, so confident had they been of reaching it, the Brazilians had booked the only aeroplane. The Italians had to travel on a jam-packed train, with most of them standing up all they way.

Then they got confused about kick-off time, reached the ground far too early and had to turn round and go back to their hotel. Maybe they were anxious to get on with the game. It was rumoured that one fanatical supporter had sent the team a telegram saying: "Win or die!"

After all this, they had every right to feel a bit dazed when they beat Hungary 4–2 to take the World Cup for the second time. Their manager, Vittorio Pozzo, certainly was. During the after-match celebrations he was so stunned he didn't realize that water from the trainer's bucket was pouring into his shoes!

Qualifying quandaries

World Cup competitions take place every four years. The next two tournaments are due to take place in 1998 and 2002. But they are only the years of the "finals" – the part of the World Cup which is played out over a period of about a month.

Before that happens, stacks of "qualifying" games have to take place. This is to decide which of the many countries who enter the World Cup are actually going to compete in the finals. It's not easy! Over the years qualifying has got harder and harder, and qualifying matches have thrown up plenty of their own wicked tales.

In the qualification matches for 1970, for instance, El Salvador and Honduras met three times, beating each other once before El Salvador went through by winning a playoff 3–2.

The matches caused so much tension that Hondurans began to attack Salvadoreans living in their country – in return for which the Honduras government launched an armed attack on Honduras! They took their football far too seriously.

The qualification quiz

Try this qualification quiz to see how wicked the business can be!

1 In 1934, Italy had to qualify – even though the finals were being held in Italy. True or false?

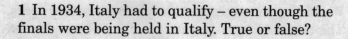

2 India qualified from the Asia group for the 1950 tournament, but then withdrew after being told – what?
a) That their footwear wouldn't be allowed.
b) That they'd have to change their shorts for longer ones.
c) That they'd have to change the colour of their shirts.

3 Wales won the African and Asian group in 1958. True or false?

4 Spain and Turkey were the only teams in their qualifying group for 1954. After each beating the other, they faced a playoff match. Before the game a forged telegram was received which caused Spain to leave their star player, Cuba, out of their team. The playoff match was drawn. What happened next?
a) Another match was played.
b) The teams tossed up.
c) Spain were awarded the game.

5 Belgium won their 1974 qualifying group without losing a match or conceding a goal. True or false?

40

6 In the Africa group for 1978, Morocco and Tunisia were level on scores at the end of two legs. The winners were decided by means of a method never before used in World Cup match. What was it?

a) Playing on until the first goal was scored.

b) Corner kicks.

c) Penalty shoot-out.

7 Fiji set a record when trying to qualify for 1982 by letting in 12 goals in three days. True or false?

8 When did the opening game of qualification for the 1998 competition take place?

a) 10 March 1995.

b) 10 March 1996.

c) 10 March 1997.

Answers:

1: TRUE. Good job they managed it! After 1934, FIFA, realizing how few spectators would turn up to watch the finals if the host country weren't taking part, decided that they wouldn't have to qualify in future. The reigning champions have never had to qualify.

2: a) India's footwear was – nothing! They wanted to play in bare feet, and FIFA rules didn't allow it.

3: TRUE! When all the other teams withdrew from this group rather than play Israel, FIFA drew lots for another team to challenge them for

---

a place in the finals. Wales won the draw and beat Israel to claim their place.

4: b) – and Turkey won!

5: FALSE – Belgium didn't lose a match or concede a goal, but they *didn't* go through. Holland did. The two countries drew 0–0 against each other, but Holland beat the other teams in their group by more goals than Belgium and so went through on goal difference.

6: c) The penalty shoot-out had never been used before. Now it's used all the time! (Tunisia and Morocco were good at drawing. They'd managed it twice before, with lucky Morocco winning the toss-up. When it came to penalties they weren't so good. Tunisia won.)

7: FALSE. They were nearly twice as bad as that! They lost 10–0 away to Australia, then two days later, lost 13–0 away to New Zealand to make it 23 goals they'd let in! (It's not a record any more, though. See 1998!)

8: b) It was between Dominica and Antigua, and the game ended in a 3–3 draw. Dominica's ground held 4000 (only 300 seats, and they were under a roof with holes in it.) A newspaper report quoted the groundsman as saying that he sometimes used goats to keep the grass down and allowed local school children to play in a goal.

Not so friendly!

Qualifying for the World Cup finals is a serious business. In the build-up to the 1958 tournament, Northern Ireland were in the same qualifying group as Italy. They were all ready to play their match in Ireland – but the referee wasn't! He'd been delayed and couldn't get there in time. Another referee was offered, but the Italians refused to accept him and insisted on the game being played another day.

They did agree to play the Irish in a friendly match, though – except that it didn't work out to be too friendly! At the end of the bad-tempered game each Irish player had to shepherd off an Italian player as the furious crowd invaded the pitch ... and the furious police chased after them!

As it happened, the Irish got their own back. When the proper match was played, they won 2–1 and Italy were eliminated. The friendly had been a draw – which would have put Italy into the 1958 finals instead!

Wicked World Cup question

The World Cup is played every four years – but who held it for over 5 years?

Wicked answer: An Italian civil servant, named Orlandi Barassi. Worried that it would be stolen when the Second World War broke out in 1939, he kept it hidden under his bed in a shoebox. When the war ended in 1945, he fished it out and gave it back to FIFA.

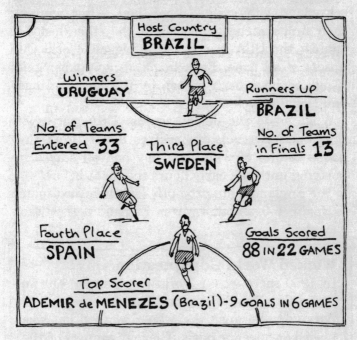

1950 URUGUAY SURPRISE

Host Country
BRAZIL

Winners
URUGUAY

Runners Up
BRAZIL

No. of Teams
Entered 33

Third Place
SWEDEN

No. of Teams
in Finals 13

Fourth Place
SPAIN

Goals Scored
88 IN 22 GAMES

Top Scorer
ADEMIR de MENEZES (Brazil) – 9 GOALS IN 6 GAMES

Hooray!

In 1950, after rejoining FIFA, England became the first British country to take part in the World Cup finals.

Boo!

It was a disaster.

FIFA had decided that the British Championship should be the qualifying group for the home countries, and that the top two teams should go to the finals in Brazil. This time it was Scotland who got all snooty. Saying that they'd only compete as British champions, they met England in a decider at

Hampden Park. England won 1–0, and Scotland stayed at home.

England only *wished* they had. After winning their first match against Chile, they then lost 0–1 against the USA in one of the biggest World Cup upsets of all time. Back home, a newspaper said: "England have been beaten by the Mickey Mouse and Donald Duck team"!

What made the defeat against USA worse was that the Americans themselves didn't think they had a chance of winning. They had all stayed up partying until the early hours the night before!

The England team promptly lost their next match to Spain, 1–0, and that was it. England were on their way home.

Wicked World Cup question

In 1950 there was a World Cup winner, but no World Cup final? How come?

Answer: Because the whole competition was played on a league basis. The four winners of the first-round groups went into another league, with the top team taking the title. It was pure coincidence that the final match, between Brazil and Uruguay, turned out to be the deciding game.

Behind them they left a tournament that had reached its final stages. The last match was Uruguay against Brazil, with Brazil only needing a draw to come top of the final group and win the cup.

As far as some people were concerned, it was no

contest. The night before the game, the Governor of the Brazilian state of Rio made a speech. Beginning "You Brazilians ..." he went on to say – what?

Answer: all of them!

It was the most wicked speech in World Cup history. The next day, Brazil went out ... and lost 1–2! Uruguay were the 1950 champions.

Nowadays we take it for granted that club and international football teams will have a manager. But that wasn't always the way, at least for England. The first manager of England was only appointed in 1946. Until then, teams were picked by a Football Association committee, whose members voted for who they wanted in the team!

Could you be an international manager? Try this quiz and see how you get on. Points are scored for good and bad decisions!

THE MANAGEMENT GAME

1 NO WORKING

Your players all have other jobs. You fix it with their employers to have time off to play in The World Cup.

Good or Bad Decision?

2 NO SHIRKING

You tell your players that you'll put them in the army if they don't play well.

Good or Bad Decision?

3 NOT STAYING

You threaten to walk home if your team lose their match.

Good or Bad Decision?

4 NOT LISTENING

Your players think you're not qualified to tell them how to play, because they're stars and you've never played International football. You shut up.

I'VE SHUT UP

Good or Bad Decision?

5 NO EXPERIENCE

ALDER SHOT

You appoint a man whose previous job was manager of Aldershot Reserves.

Good or Bad Decision?

NO WAY!

The evening before a big match you tell your team they've got no chance.

Good or Bad Decision?

NO PLAY TODAY

The law of your country says that you're not allowed to play football on a Sunday. You ignore it.

Good or Bad Decision?

I SAY!

You announce that your country WILL win the next World Cup.

Good or Bad Decision?

NO DRINKING

You shut your players up in a training camp and forbid them to go out. Then you discover they've formed an 'escape committee' to sneak off down the pub. You tell them that anyone who tries it will never play for you again!

Good or Bad Decision?

NO EATING

You're playing in a foreign country and don't trust the local food – so you take your own!

Good or Bad Decision?

NO PRACTICE

Your own F.A. have suspended many of your players because they didn't play in a club game. You say that if they don't un-suspend them you'll stop playing practice games for the World Cup.

Good or Bad Decision?

NO MORE GOALS

It's half-time in a World Cup game and your team is already 0-3 down. You decide to substitute your goalkeeper.

Good or Bad Decision?

NO SWIMMING

Before a match you say that if the team lose they should all be thrown in the Mediterranean.

Good or Bad Decision

NO GO!

One of your players stays out too late one night so you remove him from your World Cup squad.

Good or Bad Decision?

Answers:

1 Good. It's 1930 and your team is Romania. Your country don't do well, but your decision means they go down in history as having played the first ever World Cup tournament. (How did you do it? easy! You're not a real manager – you're King Carol!)

2 Good. It's 1934 and your team is Italy. You win the World Cup!

3 Good. It's 1934 and you're Dr Deitz, manager of Hungary, speaking before your team play Switzerland. They win 2–0!

4 Bad. It's 1950 and you're Walter Winterbottom, manager of England. Your team return in disgrace.

5 Good! It's 1950, the manager is George Naylor and your country is Sweden. You come third, then in 1958 Naylor leads you to the final itself.

6 Good! It's 1950, you're name is Bill Jeffrey and you're manager of USA. Your team go out next day and beat England 1–0!

7 Good. It's 1958 and your country is Northern Ireland. You surprise everybody by reaching the quarter-finals.

8 Good! It's leading up to 1966 and you're Alf Ramsey, manager of England. You *do* win it!

9 Good. This was Ramsey in 1966 too. The England players knew then that they couldn't get up to anything, so they concentrated on playing.

10 Bad. It's England manager Alf Ramsey again, but this time in 1970. Not trusting the food in Mexico, he took 63 kilos (140lbs) of burgers, 180 kilos (400lbs) of sausages, 136 kilos (300lbs) of fish and 10 cases of tomato ketchup … only for goalkeeper Gordon Banks to cry off just before the quarter-final match against Germany with – stomach trouble!

11 Good. It's 1972 and you're Cesar Menotti, manager of Argentina. Your FA get the message, reinstate the players and you go on to qualify for the 1974 finals.

12 Bad. You're manager of Zaire, playing Yugoslavia in the 1974 tournament. Your substitute goalkeeper is even worse. He lets in another six and your team loses 0–9!

13 Good *and* bad. It's 1982 and you're Jupp Derwall, manager of Germany. Your team cause a shock by losing 1–2 to Algeria, but still go on to reach the World cup final.

14 Bad. You're Tele Santana, manager to Brazil in 1986. You throw out the Flamengo player Renato Gaucho – but then his team-mate Leandro says in that case he's not playing either, so you've lost two players!

How did you get on?

Over 10 Terrific. With you in charge, a team would be potential World Cup winners!

5–10 Not so good. Your team would make the final tournament, but if you wanted to see the games in the later stages you'd need to buy a ticket!

Under 5 Awful. Your team wouldn't qualify and you'd get the sack. Never mind – you'd almost certainly be offered a job as a TV pundit and get to see all the matches anyway!

Wicked World Cup quote

Managers need to be able to come up with a good excuse when they lose. The Bulgarian manager came up with a classic after his team lost a qualifying match against Austria. "My players were not in the right frame of mind. It was dirty tricks. They hoisted a flag which wasn't ours and then played a dreadful version of our national anthem. We lost our composure."

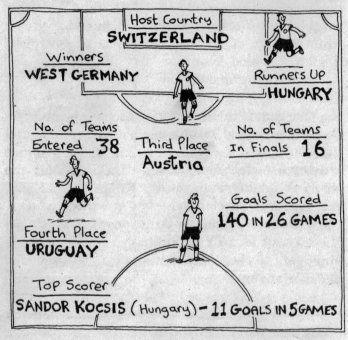

Host Country
SWITZERLAND

Winners
WEST GERMANY

Runners Up
HUNGARY

No. of Teams
Entered **38**

Third Place
Austria

No. of Teams
In Finals **16**

Fourth Place
URUGUAY

Goals Scored
140 IN 26 GAMES

Top Scorer
SANDOR KOCSIS (Hungary) **– 11 GOALS IN 5 GAMES**

England successfully qualified for the 1954 finals in Switzerland. This time they were joined by Scotland who, although the British championship was again used as the qualifying competition and they'd again come second, had swallowed their pride and accepted FIFA's invitation.

As it happens, they'd have done better to stick to their 1950s tactic and stay at home. They played two games and lost them both – to Austria 0–1, and then to Uruguay 0–7!

Wicked World Cup quote

After Scotland had lost 0–7 to Uruguay a newspaper reporter said that the Scottish defenders "stood around like Highland cattle". Mind you, he was an *English* newspaper reporter!

England did a bit better. They reached the quarter-finals thanks to a 2–0 win against Switzerland and a 4–4 draw with Belgium. It was in this match that the Portsmouth player Jimmy Dickinson hit the only goal he'd score in his 48 games for England. Pity it was an own goal!

After that, England went the same way as the Scots, losing 2–4 against Uruguay – although one of Uruguay's goals should definitely have been disallowed. Given a free kick, the Uruguayan midfielder, Varela, waited until the referee wasn't looking then picked the ball up and hammered it downfield goalkeeper-style. With the English players still rubbing their eyes in disbelief, Uruguay went through and scored!

Ooh, my head!

One of the most amazing games in 1954 was that between Austria and Switzerland, which finished 7–5! It was 5–4 at half-time, with all 9 goals scored in a period of just 24 minutes.

Part of the blame was pinned on the Swiss defender Roger Bocquet, who seemed to be playing in a trance. He was. He'd found out before the game that he was seriously ill with a tumour and needed to have an operation. His doctor had forbidden him to play but Bocquet, thinking he might not survive the operation, had decided there was no way he was going to miss playing what might be his last game!

Wicked World Cup fact

The spectators at the match between Hungary and South Korea in 1954 saw more goals than free kicks! Hungary won 9–0 but there were only 5 free kicks.

The Battle of Berne

Just about the most wicked match in World Cup history took place in 1954. It was the quarter-final match between Hungary, the tournament favourites, and Brazil. Played at Berne Stadium, it became known as the "Battle of Berne". Here are the match facts:

- One Hungarian, Bozsik, sent off. (Bet he felt sik about it!)
- Two Brazilians, Santos and Tozzi, sent off, even though Tozzi went down on his knees to plead with the referee not to do it!
- Two penalties, one for each side.
- Hungary winners, by 4–2.

That was just the match which took place on the pitch. After the final whistle blew, though, a second match began!

- A Hungarian, who hadn't been playing, hit a Brazilian with a bottle as he left the field.
- The Brazilians promptly gathered in the players' tunnel and turned the lights out.
- As the Hungarians came off the pitch the Brazilians invaded their changing room for a mass punch-up.
- Result of the second match: a draw! Not one of the players was punished, either by their countries or by FIFA.

Wicked Wonders: Ferenc Puskas and the Magical Magyars

The Hungarians of 1954 would be remembered for all the right reasons, too. They were a brilliant team – as England had discovered. In 1953 they'd been walloped by Hungary not once, but twice: 3–6 at Wembley (the first time England had ever lost an international match at home) then 7–1 in Hungary! The Hungarians were known as the "Magical Magyars" and for good reason:

Between June 1950 and November 1955 they won 43 out of 51 matches, scoring in every single game. In total they banged in 220 goals – an average of 4 goals a game.

In that time, they lost just once. Unfortunately, it was in the 1954 World Cup final! With their star player, Ferenc Puskas, not fully fit, they lost 2–3 to Germany after being 2–0 up in 8 minutes!

Wicked World Cup fact

Hungary had beaten a weak German side 8–3 in a first-round group match! After Germany's surprising win in the final, a wicked rumour spread that many of their players had been using drugs to improve their performances. This was never proved – although afterwards many of the German players were packed off to rest homes to recover from something!

Ferenc Puskas

Could one player make that much difference to a team? In the case of Puskas, the answer is "definitely!" Known as the "Galloping Major", because he was once a major in the Hungarian army, he had a phenomenal goalscoring record for his country – 83 goals in 84 internationals!

In total, Puskas scored 780 goals in 823 first class matches. Many of these were for the Spanish club Real Madrid. With him in their side, they won the European Cup (now the Champion's Cup) for the first 5 years of its existence! In one of them, Real beat Eintracht Frankfurt 8–3, with Puskas scoring 4 goals.

This is all the more surprising when you consider that Puskas was very left-footed and hardly ever used his right foot. It was said that this was partly due to coming from a very poor family as a child. His father could only afford to buy him one shoe. It fitted his right foot best, which is why he never kicked a ball with that foot – to stop his shoe wearing out! How many goals might Puskas have scored if his dad had been rich enough to buy him two shoes?

Scatty Scotland, Iffy Northern Ireland and Wobbly Wales

For both the 1950 and 1954 World Cups, the British Championship was used by FIFA to determine which two countries out of England, Northern Ireland, Scotland and Wales would qualify for the finals. The disadvantage of this was that it meant that two of the four countries would *always* be knocked out. So after 1954 things were changed to the way they are now, with the British countries mixed up amongst the different European qualifying groups.

That's when the four discovered the advantage of the old system. At least with their own group it meant that two of them always *would* qualify...

Scatty Scotland: super and sad

Scotland have definitely been super-Scotland when it comes to qualifying for World Cup finals. Out of the 11 possible finals they could have reached between 1954 and 1994, how many did they qualify for? **Answer – 7** ... better than most countries in the world.

The trouble is, they're not so good when they actually get to the finals. Out of the 7 they've played in, how many times have they been knocked out in the first round? **Answer – 7 again!** One 100% record the Scots would prefer not to have.

Here's a quick quiz about Scotland's record. Which of the following teams have they beaten in World Cup finals, and which have they lost to?

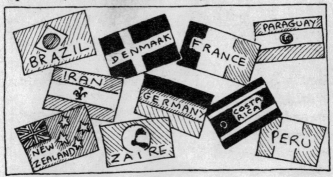

Answer: They've only beaten New Zealand (5–2 in 1982) and Zaïre (2–0 in 1974). Against all the other teams they've either lost or drawn.

Good though they are at qualifying, though, in the 1978 qualifiers they really had a stroke of luck. At 0–0 in a tense match against their nearest rivals, this is what happened:

A long ball was pumped into their opponents penalty area....

.... A group of players went up to head it...

The ball hits the hand of Joe Jordan, Scotland's centre forward, only for.....

...The referee to award Scotland a penalty!

They scored, drew 1-1 and qualified. Who were their unlucky opponents? Wales!

Wicked World Cup quote

Sometimes the Scots players don't seem to get on with each other as well as they should. A team-mate, clearly thinking that Graham Souness had a big head, said in 1978: "If he was made of chocolate he would eat himself".

Wobbly Wales and iffy Northern Ireland

If Wales hadn't had such wicked luck and had beaten Scotland to qualify for the 1978 finals, it would have doubled the number of times they'd managed to do it. Yes, sadly, out of a possible 12 finals between 1950 and 1994, Wales have an almost perfect record of failure – they've qualified just once!

Northern Ireland have done better, reaching three finals. Not bad for a team who started off their international career in 1880 by losing 0–13 to England, and who had to wait until 1887 before they won an international match against anybody!

Northern Ireland's approach to the game has always been different. Their captain in 1958, Danny Blanchflower, said: "Our tactics are to equalise before the other team scores."

Blanchflower's tactics certainly worked that year, because Northern Ireland reached the finals in Sweden.

Wicked World Cup question

Which of the other British teams also qualified in 1958?

Answer: England ... and Scotland ... and, for their only appearance, Wales! Yes, in 1958 all four British teams qualified. England and Scotland were expected to do well. Northern Ireland and Wales weren't expected to do anything at all. But it didn't quite work out that way...

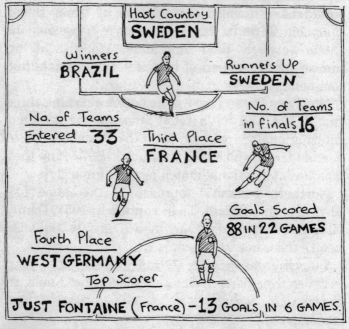

Host Country
SWEDEN

Winners
BRAZIL

Runners Up
SWEDEN

No. of Teams
Entered **33**

Third Place
FRANCE

No. of Teams
in finals **16**

Goals Scored
88 IN **22 GAMES**

Fourth Place
WEST GERMANY

Top Scorer

JUST FONTAINE (France) **– 13** GOALS IN 6 GAMES.

What actually happened was that England and Scotland *didn't* do well, but Northern Ireland and Wales *did*. Both of them reached the quarter-finals, whilst England and Scotland were knocked out after the first-round groups.

Northern Ireland eventually lost 0–4 to France, who had the all-time top scorer for the World Cup in their side. Just Fontaine scored 13 goals in the tournament, two of them against Northern Ireland.

The Irish first-choice striker wasn't so lucky. Billy Simpson, of Rangers, was injured after just five minutes' training. He didn't play a match!

Wales did even better. In their quarter-final they only lost 0–1, and that was against Brazil – the eventual champions. Their hero that day was their goalkeeper, Jack Kelsey of Arsenal, who saved everything until he was beaten by a lucky deflection.

Afterwards he told reporters the secret of his success. "Chewing gum!" said Kelsey. "I always put some on my hands and rub it well in!"

Wicked wonders: Pelé and the brilliant Brazilians

The champions in 1958 were Brazil, the first country ever to win the World Cup on a different continent to their own.

During the tournament they played 6 games and scored 16 goals. The only team they didn't beat was England, drawing 0–0 with them in their first-round group. (Unfortunately England didn't beat anybody else either, which is why they went out!)

In the final Brazil beat the host country, Sweden, 5–2 with two of the goals being scored by a 17-year-old player named Pelé. The first of these goals was a classic. Here's how to practise it in the playground:

Stand in the penalty area waiting for a cross from the wing. When the ball comes over, get to it before the player marking you and trap it on your chest...

...as the ball comes down flick it over the head of another defender rushing in to tackle you...

...as the ball comes down again don't wait for it to bounce...

... but volley it into the net! (You may need to practise this a few million times before you get it right – unless your name is Pelé the Second!)

Here are some more facts about the brilliant Brazilians.

- Brazil are the only country to have played in every single World Cup finals.
- They've won the trophy four times – in 1958, 1962, 1970 and 1994.
- They didn't lose a qualifying match for 60 years! Their defeat by Bolivia in the qualifiers in 1994 was their first ever.

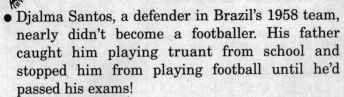

Wicked World Cup question
The first Brazilian to receive a winners' medal was Anfilogino Guarasi, in 1934 ... a year when Brazil were knocked out in the first round. How did he do it?
Answer: He was playing for Italy!

- Djalma Santos, a defender in Brazil's 1958 team, nearly didn't become a footballer. His father caught him playing truant from school and stopped him from playing football until he'd passed his exams!

- Garrincha, an amazing winger who played in the 1958 and 1962 winning teams nearly didn't become a footballer either – for a much more serious reason. As a child he'd contracted a disease which had left him with badly deformed legs. He overcame this affliction so well that in the 1962 final, when Brazil played Czechoslovakia, the man marking stopped trying to win the ball and stood watching him with his hands on his hips!

- Even Brazilian non-players are quick on their feet! The moment the referee blew his whistle to end the 1958 final, Americo, the team's trainer, raced on and stole the ball from him as souvenir!

- Because most Brazilians have incredibly complicated names, most are known by nicknames. Let's face it, if you were a TV commentator would you prefer to say "It's a great goal by Edson Arantes do Nascimento!" or "It's a great goal by Pelé!"?

Pelé – The most brilliant Brazilian of them all

Pelé is probably the most famous footballer in the world. He won three World Cup winner's medals with Brazil and countless other honours. But, if he'd had his own way, everybody would have still been calling him by his real name: Edson Arantes do Nascimento. After the other kids at school made up the nickname for him, Pelé didn't like it and would start a fight with anybody who used it. Fortunately for everybody else, this got him into so much trouble he decided it was better to keep his nickname and concentrate on his football.

Well, rag-ball rather than football. Born into a poor family, Pelé didn't have a football of his own until he was 10. Before that, he played barefoot in the streets with a ball made of rags!

Then, when he did get boots and a ball, his team didn't have a decent set of shirts. Pelé helped solve this problem himself. Trains used to pass near his home, their open wagons piled high with the peanut harvest (nuts of all sorts grow in Brazil). Not surprisingly, as the train rattled along a few peanuts would fall off. What did Pelé do? Picked them up and sold them until his team had enough money for the shirts they needed!

Leaving school at 14, he became an apprentice shoemaker (at least he'd learn how to make his own boots!) but didn't complete the apprenticeship. By then, his talent had already been recognized and a year later, when he was just 15, Pelé gave up shoemaking and became the youngest player in the Brazilian league with his club, Santos. Another year on, aged 16, he played his first international for Brazil!

His career with Santos was amazing. In 1114 games, Pelé scored an incredible 1090 goals! His 1000th goal came from a penalty.

When the referee awarded it, nobody in the crowd was left in any doubt about what was going to happen. The stadium announcer told the crowd this was going to be Pelé's 1000th goal – before he ran in to take the kick! Pelé was so popular in Brazil by then that his country even issued a special commemorative postage stamp to mark the feat.

His fame was worldwide. During one match for Santos in Colombia, the referee sent Pelé off by mistake – it should have been another Santos player. Pelé was back in the dressing room and unlacing his boots when he was told to go back out again. The huge crowd had been so annoyed at what had happened that they were setting fire to cushions and throwing them on the pitch! To avoid a full-scale riot it had been decided that Pelé must return and the referee must go. The referee's place was taken by one of the linesmen and Pelé completed the match!

Pelé made 91 appearances for Brazil, 14 of them in the final rounds of four different World Cup tournaments. In those games he scored 12 goals – but he's almost as famous for the goals he just missed.

During the 1970 tournament he almost scored from the half-way line against Peru. Then in the semi-final against Uruguay, he raced after a through ball and:

...let it run past one side of the Uruguayan's onrushing goalkeeper while....

...he ran round the other side of the goalkeeper then....

...caught up with the ball and, as a defender rushed back to cover....

....Pelé hit it past him only to shave the far post instead of scoring!

Pelé retired from the game in 1974, only to be persuaded to come back a year later to play for New York Cosmos in the newly-formed North American Soccer League (NASL). After helping Cosmos win the title, he finally retired for good in 1977 – and the NASL promptly collapsed!

Pelé became Brazil's Minister for Sport in 1994. He now spends his time touring the world as an ambassador for his country – a far cry from the 17-year-old who burst into tears at the end of the 1958 final.

Nutty nicknames

Like the Brazilians, some players are given nicknames because their real names are either too long, or too hard to pronounce. Others, though, have been given nicknames to describe the sort of players they are – and some of them have been wicked!

See if you can match the players to their nicknames in this quiz.

PLAYERS

1 GARRINCHA (BRAZIL 1958) – A speedy winger.

2 BENITO LORENZI (ITALY 1954) – Who was always arguing with the referee.

3 GEORGIO GHEZZI (ITALY 1954) – A madly diving goalkeeper.

4 LEV YASHIN (RUSSIA 1966) – A goalkeeper with long arms and an outfit that didn't show the mud.

5 SIGVARD PARLING (SWEDEN 1958) – A solid defender.

6 ALAN SHEARER (ENGLAND 1998) – A crisp striker.

7 GERHARD MULLER (WEST GERMANY 1970) – A solid attacker.

8 RYAN GIGGS (WALES, IF THEY EVER REACH THE FINALS AGAIN) – A friendly youngster.

NICKNAMES

A) POISON

B) FATTY

C) THE BLACK OCTOPUS

D) THE CORDIAL KID

Pleased to meet you.

E) LITTLE BIRD

H) SMOKY

F) KAMIKAZE

G) THE IRON STOVE

Answers: 1–e 2–a (In Italy's match against Switzerland in 1950, he argued with the referee so much that the official retaliated by disallowing a fair goal for offside!); 3–f (like the Japanese wartime pilots who would deliberately dive-bomb their aeroplanes on to ships they were attacking); 4–c; 5–g 6–h (but not because he burns up opponents – because he loves eating crisps) 7–b; 8–d (but not because he's friendly – because his favourite drink is blackcurrant cordial).

Host Country
CHILE

Winners
BRAZIL

Runners Up
CZECHOSLOVAKIA

Third Place
CHILE

No. of Teams Entered **56**

No. of Teams in Finals **16**

Fourth Place
YUGOSLAVIA

Goals Scored
89 IN 32 GAMES

Top Scorer
DRAZEN JERKOVIC (Yugoslavia) — **5 GOALS IN 6 GAMES**

Wicked World Cup fact

For the duration of the 1962 tournament every school in Chile was closed!

England were the only British team who qualified for the 1962 finals in Chile. They put up their best performance to date, reaching the quarter-finals before being beaten 1–3 by the eventual winners, Brazil.

In this game the Brazilian winger Garrincha was at his wicked best, scoring two goals and making the other. One of them was a header, for which he managed to out-jump Maurice Norman, the England defender – even though Norman was 20 cms (8 in) taller!

From there, Brazil cruised to the final where the beat Czechoslovakia 3–1 to retain the title they'd won in 1958.

Wicked World Cup question

How many footballs were matches played with in Chile?

Answer: Two!

The host country wanted the matches to be played with Chilean footballs. Unfortunately, their footballs kept going flat or losing their shape – or both! So, to spare the feelings of their hosts, referees would start the game with a Chilean football, but exchange it for a decent one the first time it went out of play!

Talking of footballs, the Brazilian trainer Americo doubled his collection in Chile. At the end of the final he raced on and swiped the ball from the referee just as he'd done in Sweden!

Medicine men

One non-footballing lesson that England learned in 1962 was to take their own doctor with them. They went to Chile without one, and it nearly cost an England player his life. Peter Swan, the Sheffield Wednesday defender, fell ill. He'd contracted dysentery, an illness that makes you go to the toilet a lot. This would have been bad enough, but when the local doctor looked at him he diagnosed Swan as having a different kind of stomach problem. What did he prescribe? A laxative – to make him go to the toilet!

Nowadays, teams have their own medical teams with them – from doctors behind the scenes to those with their boxes of tricks who run on to the pitch to deal with any player who gets injured.

Play this wicked medical game – and see if you survive!

THE MEDICAL GAME

1 BAD COLLISION - MISS A TURN. In 1930 the Paraguayan player Lino Nessi broke his leg in the match against Belgium - by colliding with a goal post!

2 KNOCK YOURSELF OUT - CARRIED BACK TO THE START! In the 1930 semi-final between Argentina and USA, the USA medical assistant was so angered by a refereeing decision he threw his medical bag on the ground, breaking a bottle of chloroform (an anaesthetic). He was carried off!

4 KNOCKED OUT BY YOUR TEAM MATES - NO GOES FOR 10 MINUTES In 1954 the Uruguayan Hohlberg equalised against Hungary - and was promptly knocked unconcious by his celebrating team mates! He had to go off and Hungary went on to win!

I wish I'd missed!

3 CALL A DOCTOR QUICKLY - HAVE ANOTHER TURN When the Brazil player Nariz broke his wrist during the 1938 Tournament he had no problem getting treatment: he was a doctor himself!

Hm!

5 IGNORE A FEVER - RUN AROUND EVEN MORE. Before the 1962 final against Czechoslovakia the Brazilian winger Garrincha had a temperature of 40°C (104°F). He played - and was 'hot stuff'!

SMASH

6 SUFFER FROM SUNBURN IN A SENSITIVE PLACE - STAY IN THE SHADE FOR 2 TURNS Mexico's high altitude and thin air, which made the sunlight more powerful, caused Bobby Charlton of England to suffer from sunburn in 1970 - on his bald patch!

CARRIED ON OVER

10 HAVE AN INJECTION – GO BACKWARDS, FAST!

Contracting tonsillitis in 1986 proved a double embarrassment for England's Trevor Steven. Firstly he had to have an injection in the bum. Secondly, because the regular doctor was unavailable another doctor was called – a woman!!

FALSE ALARM – **9**
DO NOTHING UNTIL THE NEXT DAY

Before travelling to Colorado Springs in preparation for the 1986 finals in Mexico, England manager Bobby Robson gave his players a severe warning about the dangers of sunbathing at high altitude. The moment they arrived it snowed for 7 hours non-stop, and they couldn't go out at all!

8 NOTHING LEFT TO GIVE – MISS NEXT GAME – ALMOST

In 1982 Northern Ireland's Sammy McIlroy and Sammy Nelson were selected for drugs testing after a game against Spain in boiling heat. They'd become so dehydrated they both had to spend over 2 hours in the loo, and the team almost missed their plane to the next match.

Er, can I borrow some of yours?

THE MEDICAL GAME (CONTINUED)

Tooth Hurty!

No, Mick, kick off 3 o'clock as usual.

TOOTH-ACHE NEARLY MISS A TURN

England defender Mick Mills almost missed the plane to a 1970 match against Rumania. He was at the dentist

78

WATER NEEDED — GO ROUND IN CIRCLES

Again in 1986, in the heat of Spain, Chris Waddle came on as England sub carrying 6 plastic bags of water for his team mates — only for the ball to come his way immediately. Thinking quickly, he put the bags down, beat a defender, then picked the bags up again to hand around!

11

12 ## BAD TOE — PUT YOUR FEET UP FOR A WHILE.

England Striker Gary Lineker injured his toe so badly in 1990 that he couldn't fit his foot into his boot...

...So he trained in a pair of slippers!

HAVE AN OPERATION, LOSE YOUR SHIRT, BUT WIN THE GAME AND HELP OTHERS TO WIN AS WELL!

Tostao, a member of Brazil's 1970 winning team, was only able to play because of an eye operation performed by an American surgeon. He gave the surgeon his shirt and winners medal then, after retiring from football, went on to qualify as a doctor himself!

No smoking!

Finally, everybody knows that smoking is a danger to your health. Here are two wicked World Cup tales about it.

- The England squad preparing for the 1986 finals were invited to join the "No Smoking Campaign" being run by the Health Council. When manager Bobby Robson checked up, he found only one person who did smoke – the team doctor!

- FIFA didn't set a particularly good example that year, either. They not only accepted sponsorship money from the cigarette company Camel, but allowed them to float a huge yellow cigarette balloon outside Mexico's Azteca Stadium on the day of the final.

Host Country
ENGLAND

Winners
ENGLAND

Runners Up
WEST GERMANY

No. of Teams
Entered **71**

Third Place
PORTUGAL

Fourth Place
RUSSIA

No. of Teams
in Final **16**

Goals Scored
89 IN 32 GAMES

Top Scorer
EUSEBIO (Portugal) – 9 GOALS IN 6 GAMES

This was England's year in every way. They won the World Cup but Scotland, Northern Ireland and Wales didn't even qualify for the finals.

Here's your wicked guide to England's progress to become world champions.

Before the tournament even began

● Tickets for the World Cup final were freely available. All you had to do was buy tickets for lots of other games at the same time. Compared to today's prices, they sound ridiculously inexpensive: a ticket for the cheapest part of any ground for 10 matches including the final cost just £3.87½p – that's less than 40p per game! Even the most expensive ticket, giving you a seat in the main stand for every game, worked out at only £2.55 a game!

Wicked World Cup fact

If you'd bought a souvenir programme covering all the World Cup matches including the final it would have cost you 12½p … in 1998 it would be worth about £50!

- What you couldn't get at any of the grounds was a drink in a glass bottle. To counter some of the threats of hooliganism, drinks were served in cardboard containers or paper cups, rather than in glass beakers or bottles which nasty fans could throw.

- For a while it looked as if the other thing that wouldn't be seen in a World Cup match was the trophy itself. While on display at a London stamp exhibition it was stolen. A massive police operation swung into action, only for the trophy to be found under a bush by a dog named "Pickles".

So famous did he become that, together with his owner, Pickles was allowed to attend the posh hotel celebration party after England's win. (Sadly, Pickles died not long after, accidentally strangling himself with his own lead).

● As the tournament got under way, though, it seemed that everybody in the country wanted England to win ... even the person who stole the trophy! Edward Bletchley said before attending court, "whatever my sentence is, I hope that England wins the World Cup". It didn't make the judge feel any kinder towards him. He was given two years in prison!

The opening group matches

● England's first game, and the opening game of the finals, was a terrible 0–0 draw against Uruguay. This result seemed to start a wicked trend. The opening game of the World Cup finals didn't see a goal for the next 16 years either! The three tournaments which followed

all began with 0–0 draws until Belgium broke the run by scoring against Argentina in 1982.

- England's second match against Mexico looked as if it was going the same way until the desperate Wembley crowd began to chant, "We want goals! We want goals!" Almost at once, England's Bobby Charlton raced from the half-way line to bang in a rocket shot! England went on to win 2–0.

- The final group match against France was also a 2–0 win for England. It was in this match that England's tough-tackling midfielder, Nobby Stiles, was booked for a foul ... but not by the referee! A FIFA official was sitting in the stand and he issued the caution after the match was over.

The quarter-final: England vs Argentina

- It was in this game, which England won 1–0, that Argentina's captain, Antonio Rattin, was sent off for arguing with the referee. What made this so different was that Rattin was arguing in Spanish but the referee spoke only his native German! But understanding what Rattin had said wasn't important. As the referee

explained afterwards, "I sent him off because of the look on his face"!

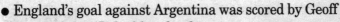

- England's goal against Argentina was scored by Geoff Hurst with a flicked header from a curling cross by his West Ham team-mate Martin Peters. They'd practised this move dozens of times at West Ham's training ground – except that, instead of real defenders, they'd used wooden posts set in concrete-filled buckets!

Semi-final: England vs Portugal

- England won this terrific match 2–1, with both goals being scored by Bobby Charlton. The second was such a cracker, a low shot that whistled into the corner of the net, that a number of the Portuguese players shook his hand as he ran back to the centre circle.

- Bobby's brother, Jack Charlton, did something in this match that he wouldn't get away with today: he deliberately handled the ball on the England goal-line to stop it going into the net. (Portugal scored from the penalty.) Nowadays he would  be sent off and miss the final. In 1966 he wasn't even booked!

World Cup final: England vs Germany

- A famous match. England were 2–1 up with seconds to go when Germany equalized. In extra time Geoff Hurst hit the bar and the linesman insisted that the ball crossed the line as it crashed down. Then, in the very last minute, Hurst staggered through and whacked in a great shot to complete his hat-trick and give England a 4–2 victory. It's a brilliant goal … isn't it?

● While all this drama was going on, the organisers were taking no chances about having the trophy stolen again! It was in a Wembley office throughout the match, being guarded by two detectives and a secretary named Sally Ellis. They had to watch the match on TV. When  it ended, the three of them had just enough time for a quick cheer before the detectives took the cup up to be presented by the Queen.

After the match

● England defender Jack Charlton was given a trophy all his own. During the tournament he'd been drawn out of the hat three times to take a random drugs test and he was picked yet again after the final. In recognition, the testers handed

Very nice, but I won't drink champagne out of it, if you don't mind!

J. CHARLTON

him a baby's potty inscribed: "presented to J. Charlton, who gave his best for his country".

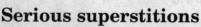

Wicked World Cup quote

Scotland player Dennis Law was not a fan of the English team. On the day of the final he went out to play a round of golf rather than watch the match on TV. On returning to the clubhouse the cheering members told him that England had won. "It was the blackest day of my life," Law said seriously.

Serious superstitions

Fancy yourself as a World Cup winner, like the England midfielder Nobby Stiles? A superstitious man, he took no chances. If you want to be like him, here's what you've got to do before the match even starts!

- wear the same shirt as for the last game that England didn't lose...
- and the same pair of cufflinks, the same tie, the same shoes, the same socks and ...
- the same underpants! (You can wash them in between games.)

Then it's time to get changed:

- put on your shorts and shirt...
- coat the inside of your boots with grease...
- soak your feet in hot water...
- then put on your socks and boots...
- before taking your shirt off again and rubbing olive oil into your chest...
- and your legs...
- before replacing your shirt...

– then knotting your tie-ups...
– and greasing your face and hands.
  Finally, you go to a mirror and...
– take off your glasses and put in your contact lenses...
– take out your false front teeth, and...
– comb your hair.

Then, if you're not too exhausted, you go out and play brilliantly!
Nobby Stiles wasn't the only England player to have superstitions...

● Whenever England stayed in a hotel, Bobby Charlton and left-back Ray Wilson were roommates. They always packed and unpacked their bags in the same fixed order: first this boot, then that one, then this shin-pad...

- Jack Charlton had a clutch of superstitions. He would change his studs at the last minute, always go on to the pitch last, and when on the pitch he would have to score during the warm up. This last ritual gave him trouble in the World Cup final because he missed the goal with his first shot! He had to grab another ball quickly so that he could bang it in!

Footballers seem to be a superstitious bunch anyway...

- Carlos Bilardo, the winning Argentine coach in 1986, certainly was. He had borrowed some toothpaste from one of his players before the first match and so did the same thing all the way through the competition. He also made his players come out and line up for the national anthem in the same order every time.

- England's Alan Shearer believes in an unusual good luck mascot – his mother-in-law! She watched him score on his England début, but didn't see the next four games when he failed to score. When she came again, he started scoring once more!

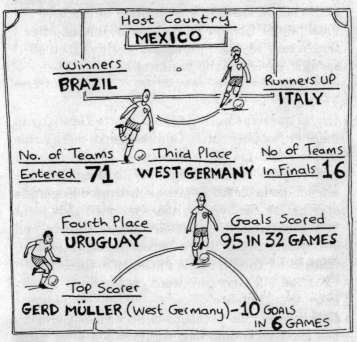

1970: BRAZIL GO NUTS

Host Country
MEXICO

Winners
BRAZIL

Runners Up
ITALY

No. of Teams Entered 71

Third Place
WEST GERMANY

No of Teams In Finals 16

Fourth Place
URUGUAY

Goals Scored
95 IN 32 GAMES

Top Scorer
GERD MÜLLER (West Germany) – 10 GOALS IN 6 GAMES

Northern Ireland, Scotland and Wales failed to qualify for the 1970 finals. England managed it – but they had a pretty simple task. As reigning champions they qualified automatically!

England managed to reach the quarter-finals, even though they were drawn in the same opening group as the eventual winners, Brazil. The match between the two teams, which Brazil won 1–0, is famous for a save made from Pelé by the England goalkeeper Gordon Banks. Sprawling on his goal-line to reach a header from the Brazilian player, Banks managed to flick it over the bar!

Wicked World Cup quote

"Goal!" That's what Pelé shouted as the ball left his head, so certain was he that he'd scored – until he saw Gordon Banks save it, that is! After this, a new saying entered the world of football-speak: "As safe as the Banks of England"!

- In the quarter-finals, England lost to Germany in another famous match. Gordon Banks wasn't able to play, and his place was taken by the Chelsea goalkeeper, Peter Bonetti. With England 2–1 ahead, manager Alf Ramsey substituted England's star player Bobby Charlton who until that point had been cancelling out Germany's captain and star player Franz Beckenbauer. (Substitutes were allowed for the first time in the 1970 finals.) With Charlton off, Germany went on to win 3–2 after extra time. Boo-hoo!

- Beckenbauer had problems of his own as Germany lost their semi-final against Italy 3–4 after extra time. He'd injured his arm late in the second half. By then, though, Germany had used their two substitutes so Beckenbauer had to play through extra time with his arm in a sling. Talk about a handicap!

92

- Italy went on to meet Brazil in the final. Both countries were aiming for their third World Cup win, which would mean being given the Jules Rimet trophy to keep for ever. Brazil won the match 4–1, took the solid gold figurine home, and kept it...

It's ours! Forever and ever and ever....

- No, not for ever. Only until 1984, when it was stolen and melted down. The famous trophy no longer exists.

Wicked World Cup fact
1970 was a red-letter year for Belgium. They won their first-ever match in the finals, 40 years after taking part in the first tournament in 1930!

Wicked wonders: the two Bobbys of England

Some great players have appeared in the World Cup for England over the years. Two of the greatest shared the same Christian name: Bobby Charlton and Bobby Moore.

Bobby Charlton was born in Ashington, in the North East of England, and learned to play the game in the back streets of his home town. He was picked to play for East Northumberland Schools. It was during a schools match that he was spotted by a Manchester United scout who reported back to the United manager, Matt Busby: "This boy could be a world-beater!"

Bobby Moore got a slightly different report. Born in the East End of London, he played for Barking and Leyton Schools. It was a West Ham scout who spotted him as a 15 year old. His report said, "This boy certainly impressed me with his tenacity and industry"; it also went on to predict, "He may not set the world alight"!

The United scout was right, the West Ham scout wrong. Both players went on to become instantly recognizable world stars – Charlton with his swerve, bullet shot and bald head, Moore with his blond hair, calm defending and immaculate appearance (when playing for West Ham he often had creases ironed down the front of his shorts, as though they were a pair of trousers!)

Bobby Charlton played for Manchester United throughout his whole career, breaking into the side when he was 19. Only fate saved him from ending his career just two years later. Returning from a European Cup match, the aeroplane carrying the team crashed when trying to take off from Munich airport. Twenty-one people died, including eight United players, but Bobby Charlton walked away with hardly a scratch. From then on he became a central figure in United's team, winning every honour in the game.

Bobby Moore went on to become West Ham's youngest captain, then, at the age of 23, captain of the England team. Moore was a terrific defender, and Pelé rated him the toughest opponent he'd ever faced. He didn't score many goals but, when he did, how did he react? He just turned round and ran back to the centre-circle for the kick-off, leaving his team-mates to get on with the hugging and kissing.

Bobby Charlton's reaction was rather different. Whenever one of his rocket shots hit the back of the net he'd leap in the air and shout, "She's there!" He scored 230 goals for Manchester United in 727 League, Cup and European Cup appearances.

One of the goals *wasn't* against Leeds United, the team his brother Jack played for. Jack was a tough defender and the boys' mother, Cissie, would often warn Jack not to kick Bobby when the two teams were playing each other. On one occasion, though, Bobby's wizardry left Jack sitting on his backside. As he leapt up and raced after his brother, Jack was heard to yell at him: "Don't even think about scoring!"

The 1970 finals were the last the two players appeared in – although, after becoming the only England captain to lift the World Cup (so far!) in 1966, Bobby Moore almost missed the 1970 tournament altogether. Before a warm-up match in Colombia on the way to Mexico, he'd been falsely accused of stealing a bracelet from a jeweller's shop in Bogota and arrested. He was only released to join the rest of the team two days later. A later investigation discovered similar cases involving other celebrities who'd visited Colombia – ranging from singers to bullfighters! Eventually, all of two years later, the guilty parties were charged with conspiracy. Maybe the police should have listened to the England squad member who pointed out that their captain didn't need to steal by saying: "Steal a bracelet? If Bobby had wanted he could have bought the whole shop!"

Bobby Moore finally ended his international career with a grand total of 108 international caps. Bobby Charlton retired after the 1970 tournament. He'd won 106 England caps. He's still England's highest goalscorer, with 49 goals.

The 100 club

Charlton and Moore may have cracked the 100-cap barrier for playing for their country, but they weren't the first – and neither of them hold the record for numbers of caps.

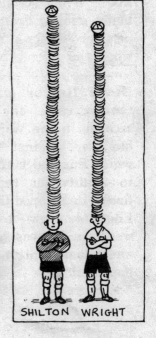

Billy Wright was the first England player to win 100 caps, eventually going on to win 105. He was England's captain, and played in the 1950 and 1954 tournaments. Amazingly for a defender, he was never booked – either for his club (Wolverhampton Wanderers) or his country!

Peter Shilton is the most-capped England player of all time with 125 caps. He played in three World Cups for England, in 1982, 1986 and 1990. He also played over 1000 league games in his career.

SHILTON   WRIGHT

The not-so-greats

No footballer gets to be picked for his country unless he's a pretty terrific player – but some who were selected for England didn't always make the biggest impact...

- **Viv Anderson** of Nottingham Forest, was in the squads for both the 1982 and 1986 finals but didn't play in a single game.
- **Phil Neal** of Liverpool once won an international cap without touching the ball. Coming on as a substitute in the dying seconds of a match against France, he'd just lined up for a free kick when the referee blew for time!
- **Kevin Hector** of Derby County came on for 90 seconds in the World Cup qualifier against Poland which England had to win to qualify for the 1974 finals. He scraped the post, England drew 1–1 and went out. It was his first and last international appearance.

Host Country
WEST GERMANY

Winners
WEST GERMANY

Runners Up
HOLLAND

No. of Teams
Entered **98**

Third Place
POLAND

No of Teams
in Finals **16**

Fourth Place
BRAZIL

Goals Scored
97 IN **38** GAMES

Top Scorer
GRZEGORZ LATO (Poland) – **7** GOALS IN **7** GAMES

Scotland were the only British country to qualify for the 1974 finals. They had a curious first round.
Record: only country out of the 16 finalists to stay unbeaten;
Result: knocked out!
Yes, although winning one game and drawing two, they came third in their group on goal difference!

Favourites to win the tournament were stylish Holland, led by their captain Johann Cruyff. He had a favourite trick for beating a defender who was marking him. Try it. The trick goes like this:

With the ball between your feet, turn sideways so that your left arm is facing the defender....

...guide the ball away from the defender with your left foot then (and this is the hard bit!)....

...flick it with the inside of your right foot so that it goes between your legs and past the defender...

.... spin round and race after it while the defender's wondering where the ball's gone.

Wicked World Cup fact
The start of the 1974 final was delayed ... because nobody had remembered to put out the corner posts!

Holland reached the final in 1974, where they met West Germany. It was a match with the most sensational start in World Cup history. The teams kicked off, Cruyff got the ball, sprinted into the German penalty area ... and was fouled. Holland scored from the penalty to go 1–0 up inside a minute! It didn't last, though. The Germans came back to win 2–1.

England were represented in this final. How? The referee who gave the first-minute penalty, Jack Taylor, came from England.

Wicked World Cup question
Which World Cup competition did "Gazza" win – on his own?
Answer: the international competition to design the successor to the Jules Rimet trophy. Engraved "The World Cup – FIFA", it is 42 cm (15 in) high, made of solid gold, cost 100,000 Swiss francs to make in 1971 ... and was designed by Italian sculptor Silvio Gazzarriga (not England's Paul Gascoigne!) It will have no permanent owner however many times any one country wins it.

Wicked wonders: 'Kaiser Franz' and Germany

Germany's overall record in the World Cup is the best of all. Here are the wicked facts about it.

- Germany have won the trophy three times (1954, 1974, 1990), been losing finalists three times (1966, 1982, 1986) and semi-finalists a further three times (1934, 1958, 1970).
- Not bad for a country which didn't have full-time professional footballers until 1963!
- They've qualified for the final tournament every time they've entered. They didn't enter in 1930, and weren't allowed to enter in 1950 because

FIFA had expelled them in 1946 following the Second World War. Who knows, they might have won both those competitions too!

- Between the 1950 and 1990 there were actually two German teams – East Germany and West Germany. The country had been divided after the war. The successful team was West Germany – and they did it using only half the players in their country!

- East Germany's record in the World Cup is pretty hopeless. Their magic moment, though, came in 1974 when they reached the final tournament and were put in the same group as West Germany. They beat the eventual winners 1–0!

- Nowadays, with Germany united again, there's just one team: Germany. It was a full German side that competed in 1994. They only reached the quarter-finals, their worst performance for 16 years!

Wicked World Cup fact

The German striker, Gerd Müller, scored 68 goals in 62 matches. Most strikers build up their tally by scoring in friendlies. Not Müller. Almost all of these goals were in European Championship or World Cup games.

Franz Beckenbauer

From trainee insurance salesman to "Emperor" of Germany – that's the story of Franz Beckenbauer, Germany's captain in 1974. Out of all the top World Cup stars, Franz Beckenbauer is unique. He's the only one who's been successful as both a player and a coach.

Aged 17, he started his full-time playing career with the German club Bayern Munich after giving up his job with an insurance company. He made his début for them at the age of 19 – on the left wing. But it *wasn't* as a winger that Franz Beckenbauer was to become so famous that the German fans would nickname him the "Kaiser" (the Emperor). The position which he made his own was that of attacking sweeper.

Not many players can claim to have invented a whole new style of play, but Franz Beckenbauer did. Until he came along, central defenders usually chose one of two options when they won the ball:

– they kicked it into the stands

– they kicked it over the stands!

Beckenbauer showed that a defender who could spring into attack could be as big a match-winner as any forward. He scored many goals, a typical example being one against Switzerland in 1966. Try this one the next time you have a big match in your street:

Franz Beckenbauer could also whack them in from a distance. Ask England – he scored one against them in 1970.

Becoming captain of both his club side and his country, Beckenbauer went on to finish his international career with 103 caps.

What then? After eight years away, some of them playing in America, he returned to become Germany's coach – and the success began again!

Under his guidance, Germany went on to appear in two more World Cup finals. They lost in 1986 but when they triumphed in 1990, Beckenbauer became the first man to have been a winner both as a player and a coach.

Host Country
ARGENTINA

Winners
ARGENTINA

Runners Up
HOLLAND

No. of Teams Entered **106**

Third Place
BRAZIL

No. of Teams In Finals **16**

Fourth Place
ITALY

Goals Scored
102 IN **38** GAMES

Top Scorer

MARIO KEMPES (Argentina) – **6** GOALS IN **7** GAMES

1978 saw the same story as 1974 as far as the British teams were concerned. Only Scotland qualified to go to Argentina, and they were knocked out in the first round – again.

In fact, the Scots team didn't have a happy time of it at all. Even their training didn't go well. One player moaned: "the training pitch takes an hour to get to, and it's so bad the cows won't eat the grass on it!"

Worse was to come. After Scotland's first match, which they lost 1–3 to Peru, their winger Willie Johnston failed a drugs test. He admitted taking pep pills and was sent home.

Scotland's one success in the competition was in beating Holland 3–2. Holland went on to reach the final. The match that put them there was against Italy. It was very nearly a disaster for the Holland defender Ernie Brandts...

– In the 20th minute, Brandts scored an own goal...
– at the same time injuring his goalkeeper, who had to be substituted!
– 30 minutes later, Brandts scored again – this time into the Italians' goal to make the score 1–1.
– Holland went on to win the game 2–1.

Argentina reached the final in a controversial way. In 1978 the second round was played in league groups, not as a knockout, with the top teams in each group going into the final. Argentina went into their last group match needing to beat fellow South American country Peru by at least 4–0; if they didn't, Brazil would go into the final. What happened? Argentina, amazingly, won 6–0! Afterwards it was claimed that the Argentine government had bribed the Peru players to lose. In retaliation, some Argentine newspapers claimed that it had been Brazil who'd been offering bribes to Peru – to play well!

The final that nearly didn't happen

Argentina may not have been guilty of bribery, but they definitely tried some wicked tactics at the start of the final…

- The team stayed behind in the changing rooms for several minutes, leaving Holland to be jeered at by the massive crowd.
- Then, just as the match was about to kick off, they complained that a plaster cast being worn by Holland's Rene Van der Kerkhof was dangerous and that he shouldn't be allowed to play (even though he'd been wearing it for ages). The issue was only sorted out when the Dutch players

107

threatened to go off and leave the Argentinians to play the final on their own! Maybe they should have. Argentina went on to win the game 3–1.

The terrible telly

The 1930 World Cup competition was watched by 434,500 spectators – and 0 TV viewers! Television coverage wasn't available. Nowadays, of course, television audiences are massive. The 52 games in the 1994 final tournament in the USA were expecting to draw a total audience of 31 billion, with 2 billion watching the final itself!

But is it always a good thing to have the World Cup matches on TV? Try your hand at this wicked TV quiz to find out!

1 In 1994, Russian policemen were happy for the matches to be on TV. Why?
2 In 1978, Italy played England in an afternoon qualifying match but neither the Italian nor the English TV companies dared show the game live. Why not?
3 During the 1986 finals in Mexico, the players would have been happier if the games hadn't been on TV. Why?
4 In 1994 a security guard in Thailand wished he'd left his TV turned off instead of

watching a match. Why?

5 A Frenchman wanted to watch a game on TV in 1982, but his wife wanted to talk. What went off?

6 Referees didn't have a lot of time for TV in 1986. Why not?

7 The citizens of Bangladesh wanted their TVs on in 1990, but they weren't. What did they do instead?

8 In Khartoum the electricity companies flashed a message across TV screens telling viewers there'd be power cuts unless they could reduce the demand for electricity in some other way. What happened?

9 Two people in Germany were glad the TV was on for Germany's match against Bulgaria in 1994, even though they didn't want to watch. Why not?

10 Again in 1994, the government in Iran were happy for TVs to be on, but not so happy about something else being off. What?

Answers:

1 The crime rate dropped by 70% as crooks stayed in to watch the matches!

2 They thought too many people would take time off work to watch.

3 The time of day when the TV companies said they'd get the biggest worldwide audiences just happened to be the hottest time of the day in Mexico. It was a case of the players overheating instead of the TVs!

4 While he watched, bank robbers carried out a safe filled with money!

5 What went off was a gun. The woman got so annoyed at her husband for not answering her questions that she shot him. Talk about a deadly shot!

6 The "time" was the extra added on for stoppages. It was claimed that FIFA told them to keep it down to save the TV companies money on satellite bookings!

7 Had a riot. The TVs weren't on because of a power breakdown, so everybody went out and attacked the power station instead.

8 The whole city was immediately plunged into darkness as everybody turned off everything except their TVs!

9 They were prisoners, and they were too busy escaping from their cell using bed sheets while their warders watched the match.

10 Spectators' clothing! They weren't happy about viewers in Iran seeing women wearing shorts and sun-tops whenever the cameras turned to show the crowd. So, they inserted their own crowd shots – of spectators dressed in fur coats! A real turn-off!

Wicked words

Wherever the TV cameras are, not far away you'll find a panel of crazy commentators and pitiful pundits to tell the viewers what they think. At least, that's the way it's been since 1970. That was the year when the first ever World Cup panel was used by ITV.

The panel started off with three members: Pat Crerand, formerly of Manchester United and Scotland; Malcolm Allison, coach at Manchester City; and Derek Dougan, formerly of Wolverhampton Wanderers and Northern Ireland.

When England were knocked out, the panel were joined by a member of the England squad who'd flown back from Mexico – Arsenal's Bob McNab. By then, though, the other three had got used to talking a lot. Poor McNab couldn't get a word in. The TV producer solved the problem by giving him a little flag to wave. When McNab flapped it, the other three panel members had to shut up!

Here are some wicked words from people who might wish they hadn't opened their mouths:

● As one player shaped up to take a free kick during

a game in the 1994 tournament, BBC pundit Trevor Brooking said:

He's going to chance his arm with his left foot.....

● During the same tournament, Brooking's fellow BBC commentator John Motson pointed out before one match that:

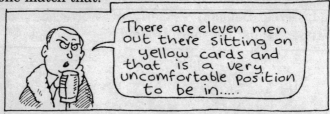

There are eleven men out there sitting on yellow cards and that is a very uncomfortable position to be in.....

● Commentators can get very excited. When Norway beat England in a 1982 qualifying match, the Norwegian commentator went completely bonkers, yelling at the top of his voice:

Lord Nelson, Sir Winston Churchill, Henry Cooper, Lady Diana, Maggie Thatcher, — Your boys took one hell of a beating!!

● No player is above criticism, even the Brazilians. In 1982, one critic didn't think much of the player Serginho's ball control, saying,

When Serginho plays, the ball is square.

When the player was taken off during a game against Italy the critic said,

● At least that critic knew who he was grumbling about. Some commentators can't always manage that. Scottish commentators Bob Crampsey and Iain Archer were covering a match between Scotland and Bulgaria when Crampsey realized that he didn't know who one of the Bulgarian players was...

Wicked World Cup fact
Before the 1996 qualifying match between England and Georgia, the two countries media teams had a "friendly" match of their own. During the game ex-England star Trevor Brooking was badly fouled and punched in the eye when he complained! He had to have his eyebrow stitched up before he could commentate on the real England against Georgia match!

● In 1994, when asked whether Brazilian players Romario and Bebeto would have been good enough to get into the famous team in which he played, Carlos Alberto, captain of Brazil in 1970 said:

Yes, but only on the bench.

● Again in 1994, when World Cup débutantes Saudi Arabia pulled off a surprise win against Morocco, their midfielder Fuad Amin crowed,

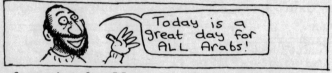

Today is a great day for ALL Arabs!

– forgetting that Morocco is also an Arab country!

Naughty newspapers

When it comes to wicked words, though, you can't beat a newspaper!

● One newspaper nicknamed ex-England manager Graham Taylor "turnip". After England lost a European Championship international to Sweden the headline was "Swedes 2 Turnips 1"!

● Sir Alf Ramsey, manager of England's triumphant 1966 team, wrote in a newspaper that Glen Hoddle, Peter Reid, Ray Wilkins and John Barnes were not good enough to be picked for a 1992 World Cup qualifying match. A few days later he listed his preferred squad in a different newspaper. He chose Hoddle, Reid, Wilkins and Barnes!

● Kamal al-Ganzuri, Prime Minister of Egypt, tried to have the Egyptian team removed from the newspapers. So angry was he after their 1997 qualifying round defeat by Ghana that he asked press not to mention the team for the remainder of their qualifying ties. His plan failed in a spectacular fashion. The countries biggest newspapers splashed the row across their front pages instead!

Wicked World Cup quote
Not all players talk directly to the media. Some still prefer to write letters. Macedonian international Mile Hristovski, wanting to find an English team, sent details of his ability to clubs in a letter. It began: "I was one of the greatest talents in football. Opposing players absolutely had not any chances…" and ended, "I would like to emphasize that I am a very modest man, not boastful." Needless to say, it made the newspapers!

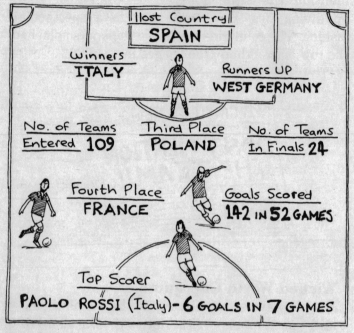

Host Country
SPAIN

Winners
ITALY

Runners Up
WEST GERMANY

No. of Teams Entered **109**

Third Place
POLAND

No. of Teams In Finals **24**

Fourth Place
FRANCE

Goals Scored
142 IN 52 GAMES

Top Scorer
PAOLO ROSSI (Italy) – **6 GOALS IN 7 GAMES**

Things went wrong for this tournament from the very beginning – at the draw ceremony to decide which teams would be in which groups! The idea was that little footballs containing the names of the countries would be pulled out of drums. Unfortunately the wrong balls were put into the wrong drums; then when the first countries were pulled out they were put in the wrong groups; finally one ball broke, preventing any more balls being drawn until it was prised out!

Once the football got under way, England, Scotland and Northern Ireland managed to qualify for the finals. Once in Spain, Scotland managed to do their usual trick and fail to win through from the first-round groups. England and Northern Ireland did a little better, getting as far as the second round. Both did something notable, though.

• Northern Ireland introduced the youngest-ever World Cup player into their team, 17-year-old Norman Whiteside of Manchester United.

• England scored the quickest-ever goal in a final tournament, skipper Bryan Robson taking just 27 seconds to score against France.

Wicked World Cup quote
When short England winger Steve Coppell tried to tackle the giant German defender Hans-Peter Briegel in their 1982 second-round match, Briegel simply sniffed, "Get away, little fly."

The tournament wasn't terribly entertaining – especially the first round match between Germany and Austria. Before the start the teams knew that a 1–0 win for Germany would allow both of them to go through to the next round of the competition. So when Germany went ahead after 10 minutes, that was that. Both teams spent the remaining 80 minutes drifting about the pitch and not attempting to score. The French manager Michel Hidalgo, who'd gone to the game to spy on the two teams, suggested that they should be awarded the Nobel Peace Prize!

Hidalgo's team themselves had an eventful time. In a first-round match against Kuwait their opponents had threatened to walk off after a whistle from the

117

crowd had stopped them playing and France had scored. Only the intervention of a member of the Kuwaiti royal family, in the shape of Prince Fahid, had persuaded them to continue – well, that and the referee changing his mind and disallowing the goal!

Then, when France met Germany in the semi-final, another wicked incident took place. Harald Schumacher, the German goalkeeper, flattened the French player Patrick Battiston with a forearm smash as the Frenchman raced towards his goal. Battiston lost two teeth and ended up in hospital, whilst Schumacher wasn't even sent off. What's more, when the match went to a penalty shoot-out (the first game in the finals ever to be decided this way) Schumacher saved two penalties to send his team into the final.

There, Germany lost 1–3 to Italy and another wicked player. The clinching goal for Italy was scored by Paulo Rossi. He'd only recently completed a two-year suspension after being involved in a plot to fix the scores of matches in the Italian league.

Wicked celebrations!

Footballers like to celebrate – when they score a goal, when they win a match or, in the case of some teams, for any reason at all…

- Although the Northern Ireland squad didn't win anything, they thoroughly enjoyed themselves. Writing in his autobiography, goalkeeper Pat Jennings said that their players invariably returned from drugs testing in a merry mood. They'd all sweated so much in the Spanish heat that they'd had to tell the officials they couldn't go to the loo. Hearing this, the officials had been forced to give them bottles of beer and lager to help out! At least, the Irish players had *said* they couldn't go…

- England's celebrations had been a bit quieter, even when they scored a goal. The chairman of the FA, Sir Harold Thompson, had written a newspaper article in which he criticized players for kissing each other!

- He'd have been in trouble with the Hungarian team. In a first-round match in 1982 they beat El Salvador 10–1, the only time a team has reached double figures in a match in the finals. Three of the goals were scored in the space of ten minutes by Hungary's substitute. His name? Laszlo Kiss!

Host Country
MEXICO

Winners
ARGENTINA

Runners Up
WEST GERMANY

No. of Teams
Entered 121

Third Place
FRANCE

No. of Teams
In Finals 24

Fourth Place
BELGIUM

Goals Scored
132 IN 52 GAMES

Top Scorer
GARY LINEKER (England) – 6 GOALS IN 5 GAMES

England, Scotland and Northern Ireland qualified for the 1986 finals, but only England made it past the first-round groups.

Northern Ireland, after starting brilliantly with a goal after just 6 minutes of their first match, managed only a draw and two defeats.

Scotland's performance was the same: one draw and two defeats. Once again, they'd performed poorly. Even their draw, 0–0 against Uruguay, wasn't a good result – they'd only had to play against ten men because a Uruguayan defender had been sent off in the first minute!

England managed to reach the quarter-finals. After a shaky start, losing to Portugal and drawing with Morocco, a Gary Lineker hat-trick against Poland put them through to the next round. Two more goals from Lineker in a 3–0 win over Paraguay put them into an infamous quarter-final match against Argentina.

Wicked World Cup question

Who lasted the shortest amount of time as England captain?

Answer: Ray Wilkins. When skipper Bryan Robson was carried off injured against Morocco in 1986, Wilkins took over the captain's armband. Less than ten minutes later, Wilkins was sent off after throwing the ball at the referee!

Argy-bargy!

England lost against Argentina, 1–2, both of the goals being scored by the Argentinian star forward Diego Maradona. It was his first goal that caused all the controversy. This is what happened:

The ball spun high in the air in England's penalty area...

....England goalkeeper Peter Shilton raced out to fist it away...

...Maradona raced in

....and fisted it himself! Into the goal!

Amazingly neither the referee nor the linesman saw anything wrong and the goal was allowed! Two minutes later Maradona scored again, racing past four England defenders in a run from the half-way line before waltzing round Shilton to pop the ball into the net.

Wickedest World Cup quote ever!

Asked about his punched goal after the match, Maradona refused to admit that he'd committed a handball – even though the TV cameras showed it clearly. "It was a little bit of the hand of God, a little bit of the head of Maradona."

With Maradona playing brilliantly, Argentina went on to become champions for the second time, beating Germany 3–2 in the final.

Let us in!

Perhaps England would have preferred the match to

be played a day earlier – then they wouldn't have been let in!

When the team turned up at the Aztec Stadium expecting to hold a training session they found the changing rooms locked. They couldn't go out to test the pitch either because it was being marked out and the grass cut. They had to go to another stadium – and only managed to get into that one thanks to their police escort calling in somebody to pick the lock on the gate!

Not that England were the first country to have stadium problems...

Non, non!
France actually withdrew from the 1950 finals in Brazil after hearing that they'd be required to play their first match in one stadium and their next game at a different stadium – two thousand miles away!

Hang on, nearly finished!
Uruguay, host country for the first ever World Cup competition in 1930, insisted on playing their opening game in their new stadium – which wasn't yet finished. They played their first match five days after everybody else!

Feeling blue

The massive Maracana stadium in Brazil – which still holds the record for a World Cup final attendance at 199,850 – was designed with special anti-hooligan measures. The seats were painted blue, because this colour was thought to have a calming influence on people!

Wicked wonders: Diego Maradona and Argentina

Argentina's record in the World Cup has been outstanding in recent years. After losing the 1930 final to Uruguay, they did very little for the next forty years. Then, suddenly, the team sprang to life to become champions in 1978 and 1986, and runners-up in 1990.

The one thing that has been consistent about them, though, is controversy.

● They withdrew from the 1938 finals in retaliation against FIFA for choosing France as hosts instead of them.

● They withdrew from the 1950 finals in Brazil, this time after an argument with the Brazilian FA.

● In 1958 they were walloped 1–6 by Czechoslovakia and pelted with rubbish by their fans when they got home.

● In 1966, even before their infamous game with England, they'd had their defender, Albrecht, sent off for a rugby tackle in their first-round game with Gemany.

● Then, as defending champions in 1982, they reached the second round only to be knocked out after two dreadful matches. In the first they lost 1–2 to Italy, the Italians having two players booked for kicking lumps out of the Argentine's star player and Argentina themselves doing even worse by having three players booked and one sent off. They then lost to Brazil, 1–3, this time with their star player being sent off himself.

And who was this star player? None other than that "handiest" of performers, Diego Maradona.

Maradona

Very few players in the world can have had a more amazing, up-and-down career than Diego Armando Maradona.

Born in Buenos Aires in 1960, Maradona became famous throughout Argentina as a 9-year-old ball-juggler! His brilliant ability at doing tricks with a football gave him a regular spot on a TV programme and he was seen nationwide.

Although he'd been playing matches with a junior team, Maradona then got together

125

with some friends to form a team of their own. They called themselves "The Little Onions" – probably because they always ran rings round the opposition! They must have been good because the whole team were promptly signed up by the professional club, Argentinos Juniors.

Although part of a group, Maradona was the star. Leaving school at the age of 13, he became an Argentinos Juniors player and made his debut with them at the age of 15. Just a year later, aged 16½, he played his first international!

Then came the first of his set-backs. Unexpectedly, the Argentine manager dropped him from his squad just before the 1978 finals. Maradona didn't speak to him for months afterwards. Plenty of people in the country continued to criticize the decision as well, even though Argentina had become world champions.

His career recovered quickly. He was in the winning team when Argentina won the World Youth Cup and then, still a teenager, he moved to the Boca Juniors for £1 million.

Then it was time for a down-turn. Maradona had a bad 1982 World Cup, being kicked at every turn and sent off in the final game. Immediately after the tournament he came back up again, though, moving to Barcelona of Spain for a then-record fee of £3 million.

Maradona was about to enter the best spell of his career. In 1984 he left Barcelona for the Italian club Napoli for another world record fee of £5 million. Within two weeks, the club had got their money back, with interest – a flood of fans had bought 70,000 season tickets! In his seven seasons with Napoli, Maradona helped them to two Italian league titles and a UEFA Cup victory.

Then came the 1986 World Cup victory with Argentina, in which he was voted Player of the Tournament.

His "Hand of God" goal against England dented Maradona's reputation, but his second goal showed what a wonderful player he was:

Picking up the ball in
his own half he took
it between two
England players....

...raced into the
England half and
cut inside a third
England player...

...dribbled up to the
England penalty
area and past a
fourth England player...

... then round the
England goalkeeper...

...and stuck the
ball into the net!

All with his favourite
left foot!

From then on, it seemed, Maradona's career became
a lot more down than up.

● He captained his side to the 1990 World Cup final,
but Argentina lost and had two players sent off.

● Then, in 1991, he was arrested for taking drugs
and banned from football for 15 months.

● A comeback in Spain wasn't successful, so he
returned to Argentina. There he became captain
again – only to fail a drugs test in the 1994 finals
and be sent home in disgrace.

Another ban followed and it seemed as if Maradona's career was finally over. But...

At the time of writing he's in strict training for the 1998 finals in France. Maybe the former "little onion" is going to spring up again!

Wicked referees

The referee who missed Maradona's infamous "hand of God" goal was Ali Bennaceur, from Tunisia. England against Argentina had been his first game as World Cup referee. It also proved to be his last. For some reason he was never given another match to referee!

Wicked World Cup question

Who is the only referee the history of the World Cup who could honestly claim that he was perfect? The referee from Scotland in the 1954 finals whose name really was ... Edward C. *Faultless*!

It's easy to blame the poor old referee, of course, but could you do better? Try this wicked "what happened next" quiz

1 At the start of a match in 1930, the referee was seen wearing a jacket, shirt and tie. What did he do next?

a) Ask the way to the changing rooms.

b) Look for somebody in the crowd to be a linesman.

c) Blow his whistle to start the game.

2 In the 1930 match between France and Argentina, the referee blew for time six minutes early with France attacking dangerously. What happened next?

a) The match was declared over.
b) The teams came back to play the six minutes they'd missed.
c) France were awarded a goal.

3 In 1970 red and yellow cards were used for the first time. During the tournament, how many players were sent off for getting two yellow cards in a match?
a) 0
b) 5
c) 12

4 In the 1970 match between El Salvador and Mexico, El Salvador protested against a Mexican goal by refusing to kick off again. What did the referee do?

a) Send off the El Salvador captain.
b) Blow his whistle for half-time.
c) Change his mind and disallow the goal.

5 In 1970, Welsh referee Clive Thomas was in charge of the match between Sweden and Brazil. He looked at his watch, saw that the 90 minutes were up and blew his whistle. What happened next?

a) Play carried on.
b) Brazil scored.
c) He was mobbed.

Wicked World Cup question
Who is the only "woman" to have refereed in the World Cup finals?
Answer: Olive Thomas. That's how a misprint in the official FIFA list renamed Welsh referee Clive Thomas!

6 In 1970, the referee had just started the second half of the West Germany v Morocco match when he had to stop it again. Why?

a) He couldn't find his watch.
b) He couldn't find his linesmen.
c) He couldn't find all the players.

7 In the 1982 match against Kuwait, England player Paul Mariner was given a yellow card. What for?

a) Pushing the referee.
b) Shouting at the referee.
c) Kissing the referee.

8 In Italy's 1982 match against Peru, the Italian defender Claudio Gentile was lucky not to have a penalty awarded against him. Why wasn't it?
a) Because the ref was holding his stomach.
b) Because the ref was rubbing his eye.
c) Because the ref was gasping for breath.

9 In the dying minutes of the match against Argentina in 1990, England's John Barnes took a free kick on the edge of the penalty area. What did the referee say to him afterwards?
a) "Bad luck!"
b) "Sorry, sorry!"
c) "What a load of rubbish!"

10 In 1990, Czechoslovakia's Lubomir Moravcik was sent off against Germany. What for?
a) Kicking the ball in the air.
b) Kicking a boot in the air.
c) Kicking a German defender in the air.

Answers:
1 c) That's how referees dressed in 1930. They also wore trousers, which they tucked into their socks.
2 b) But there were no more goals.
3 a) The idea of the cards was to avoid confusion

between referees and players who didn't speak the same language, but it appeared to make matters even more confused. There were cases of players receiving more than one yellow card in a match without being sent off!

4 b) And the second half kicked off as normal.

5 a), b) and **c)**! Thomas had blown his whistle just as the Brazillians had taken a corner. Then they scored, but Thomas refused to allow the goal, and he was mobbed. He pointed out that it was their own fault – the Brazilian winger had delayed taking the corner to have an argument with the linesman about where to put the ball!

6 c) He'd restarted the game without checking that all the players were on the pitch. Some of the Moroccan team were still coming out of the changing room!

7 a) When a pass intended for Mariner got stuck between the ref's feet, the England player hauled him away to get at the ball!

8 a) and **c)** Moments before, the ball had hit the ref in the stomach and winded him. He was still recovering when Gentile committed his foul.

9 b) The referee had positioned himself on the end of the Argentine defender's wall – and Barnes' free kick had hit him!

10 b) It was in his own boot! His boot had come off when he was roughly tackled in the Germans' penalty area. When his appeal for a penalty was turned down, Moravcik kicked his boot in the air in disgust. The referee decided this was dissent, so he gave him his second yellow card of the match – and off Moravcik went!

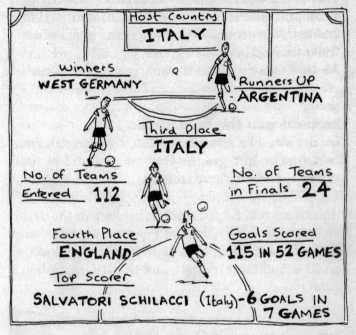

Host country
ITALY

Winners
WEST GERMANY

Runners Up
ARGENTINA

Third Place
ITALY

No. of Teams
Entered **112**

No. of Teams
in Finals **24**

Fourth Place
ENGLAND

Goals Scored
115 IN 52 GAMES

Top Scorer
SALVATORI SCHILACCI (Italy) - **6 GOALS IN 7 GAMES**

Scotland and England qualified in 1990. For Scotland it was another year of disappointment; for England, even more so but for a different reason.

The Scots yet again failed to survive beyond the first-round group, beating Sweden, but losing to Brazil and – a shock – to Costa Rica in their opening game, 1–0. In some ways that single goal shouldn't have been scored. During a lull in the play, the Costa Rican coach drew a diagram to show one of his forwards, Geovanny Jara, what he wanted to happen. Minutes later, Costa Rica scored – and it was Jara who made the goal!

Wicked World Cup fact

It was a match of mixed feelings for the Biyick brothers when Cameroon sensationally beat holders Argentina 1–0 in the opening game of the 1990 finals. Kana Biyick was sent off ... but his brother Omam scored the only goal of the match!

England win the free kicks...

Two draws and a win saw England go through from their first-round group. One of the draws was against the Republic of Ireland, managed by one of England's 1966 winning team, Jack Charlton.

In this match, England got a free kick in the dying minutes of the game. Stuart Pearce stepped up and whacked it into the net ... only to discover that the free-kick had been indirect and that the goal didn't stand!

Wicked World Cup fact

David O'Leary, the Arsenal defender, played for less than 30 minutes in the 1990 tournament but still managed to be a hero. Coming on for his only appearance as substitute in extra-time during the Republic's second round match against Romania, he hit the winner when the match went to a penalty shoot-out.

Another free kick decided England's second-round game, against Belgium. Awarded in the last minute of extra time, Paul Gascoigne chipped it forward for David Platt to volley into the net for the winner.

... then pay the penalty!

Against the Cameroons in the quarter-finals it was extra time again, and a matter of penalties. After being 1–2 down, Gary Lineker scored two penalties to put England into the semi-final against Germany.

Wicked World Cup quote

Classic quote from Bobby Robson after England reached the semi-final: "We've got here, but I don't know how."

In the semi-final the penalties went the wrong way. A 1–1 draw after extra time meant a penalty shoot-out. Stuart Pearce and Chris Waddle both missed theirs, and England had lost!

Germany went on to beat Argentina 1–0 in the final. The Argentinians had reached the final with the help of another Maradona handball, this time at the other end of the pitch. In their match against Russia, the referee hadn't seen him stop a Russian shot with his hand!

Wicked World Cup fact
Both the 1990 semi-finals were decided by penalty shoot-outs, Germany beating England and Argentina beating Italy.
So the final could easily have been England against Italy!

Wicked fans

The organizers of the 1990 tournament were seriously worried about the hooligans who followed England, so they hit on what they thought was a brilliant solution. They put England's group on the island of Sardinia so that if there was any trouble the fans would be trapped and unable to escape from the police – unless they could swim *really* fast!

Wicked World Cup quote
Security was pretty tight in Spain in 1982 as well, as England's goalkeeper, Peter Shilton, remembered: "We had a lot of security guards with machine guns around the hotel. We went to the training ground on the first day and there was a tank parked in the drive."

Thankfully, very few fans go to matches to cause trouble. Some are a bit on the wicked side, though. So, if you plan to be an international footballer one day, here are the ten most wicked types of supporters to watch out for...

1 The Hair Hauler: When Czechoslovakia went 1–0 up in the 1934 World Cup final against Italy, some Italian fans seized a Czech player's hair through the wire netting surrounding the pitch and only let him free when a rifle-carrying soldier raced to his rescue!

2 The Tomato Tosser: Returning home after coming bottom of their group in 1958, Argentine fans were waiting at the airport to pelt the team with rubbish. The same thing happened to the Italian team in 1966 after their defeat against North Korea.

3 The Bottle Bunger: Brazilian star Garrincha, sent off against home country Chile in 1962, was hit by a bottle as he left the pitch.

4 The Horn Honker: In 1970, a large group of fans spent the night before England's match with Brazil honking their car horns outside their hotel in a bid to keep the players awake.

5 The Souvenir Snatcher: At the end of the 1970 final, Brazilian fans looking for souvenirs stripped their midfield player Tostao. He lost everything except his shorts!

6 The Loo-bag Lobber: Political problems meant that

when the USA played a qualifier for the 1998 competition in Guatemala, the home crowd were not in a good mood. USA goalkeeper Kasey Keller discovered this when he was pelted with plastic bags that the fans had filled up in the loo!

7 The Cheer Chanter: Swedish fans had been whipped up by cheerleaders as their team fought its way to the 1958 final. Then FIFA banned them, the crowd was much quieter – and Sweden lost to Brazil.

8 The Pitch Pouncer: After England had taken the lead in their match against Argentina in 1966, a fan ran onto the pitch – and straight into a punch from the Argentinian left-winger, Oscar Mas.

9 The Game Gambler: An Albanian man wagered his wife on the result of Argentine's match against Romania. He lost the bet – and his wife!

10 The Pedal Pusher: So anxious to see England play in the 1982 finals was supporter Clive Tranchant that he cycled the 1000 miles from Sussex to Spain wearing an England shirt and a Union Jack cloak!

Then there are the truly terrible examples of Colombian "fans" in 1994. A few hours before their team's match against the USA, Colombian terrorists faxed their own team selection to the Colombian coach, Francisco Maturana. They warned him that he and the family of Gabriel Gomez, a midfield player, would be blown up if Gomez played. Gomez was left out, and the team lost the match 1–2.

Even worse, one of the USA goals was an own goal by the Colombian defender Andres Escobar. When the team returned home, Escobar was shot dead by an enraged supporter who snarled at him, "thanks for the own goal".

It's not always the fans who cause the players trouble though. Sometimes it's the other way round. In 1954, the Uruguayan players drove their fellow hotel guests mad by continually playing at top volume a record which said how good they were!

The other guests have begged us not to play it again. So..... let's hear the 'B' side!

Non-wicked world cup fan quote
When the Republic of Ireland reached the quarter-finals in 1990, the game was played in Rome. There the team were introduced to Pope John Paul II – except for manager Jack Charlton. When he stepped forward the Pope said, "I know who you are, you're the boss!"

141

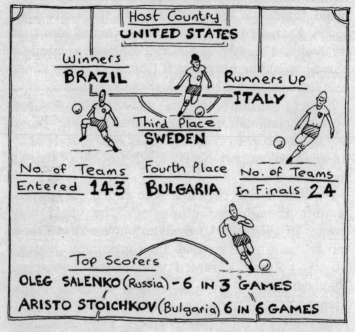

Host Country
UNITED STATES

Winners
BRAZIL

Runners Up
ITALY

Third Place
SWEDEN

No. of Teams Entered **143**

Fourth Place
BULGARIA

No. of Teams In Finals **24**

Top Scorers

OLEG SALENKO (Russia) - **6 IN 3 GAMES**

ARISTO STOICHKOV (Bulgaria) **6 IN 6 GAMES**

England didn't qualify for the 1994 finals. Neither did Northern Ireland. Nor Scotland. Nor Wales! The only United Kingdom "interest" was provided by the Republic of Ireland team managed by England's 1966 World Cup winner Jack Charlton. They managed to fight their way through the first round before being beaten by Holland.

Before the tournament began, many people questioned the decision to hold it in America – a country where, in a classic piece of bad counting, BBC radio commentator said "football is the fourth most popular sport in America" – and went on to give *four* sports that were more popular! "American football, baseball, basketball and ice hockey".

However, although there were some daft incidents – such as 20 American fans walking out of the opening match of the tournament when Germany scored against Bolivia because they thought a match ended once a goal was scored! – crowds were huge and the tournament a great success.

Wicked World Cup fact
Before the tournament began the organizers advertised for security staff, asking applicants to include a thumbprint along with their details. These were then checked against police files – and the thumbprints of 57 wanted criminals discovered! They were all promptly arrested!

The biggest sensation was the expulsion of Diego Maradona. After playing brilliantly in Argentina's two opening games, he failed a drugs test and was banned from the rest of the competition. This prompted a fan in Bangladesh to take the FIFA president, Joao Havelange, to court, saying that he'd acted illegally and ruined the World Cup for the 20,000 children in the Bangladesh branch of Maradona's fan club.

The tournament itself was won by Brazil, who beat Italy 0–0 in the final! Yes, for the first time in World Cup history, the winners didn't win the final and the losers didn't lose. Still drawing after extra time, the two teams settled the match on a penalty shoot-out which Brazil won.

Wicked World Cup question
Which 1994 team looked like a herd of elephants until they started playing?
Answer: The champions, Brazil. Before their games the players filed on to the pitch elephant-style, each of them holding hands with the player in front and the player behind.

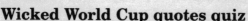

Wicked World Cup quotes quiz
With media interest in the 1994 World Cup greater than ever before, there was a truly international crop of wicked quotes. Try to match the quote with the country in this quiz!

Wicked World Cup quote	Country
a) "I do not like for me or my players to be called dogs."	1 Nigeria
b) "Any player not inspired by that atmosphere should go and play golf with his grandmother."	2 Germany
c) "Finishing second will be like finishing last."	3 Rep. Ireland
d) "We're not from the Gobi Desert!"	4 Colombia
e) "Today, God is..."	5 USA
f) "I'd say I found the winning scheme. We have ten or even nine players."	6 Spain
g) "I told my players to run around more and create a draught".	7 Bulgaria
h) "It's a shame the law allows only two substitutions. Otherwise I would have replaced all eleven players for the second half."	8 Italy
i) "And the steam has gone completely out of their sails."	9 Brazil

Answers: a)-5, said a confused Bora Milutinovic, the USA coach, after a journalist asked him how he felt about his team being considered the underdogs of their group!; **b)-1**, said Clemens Westerhof, the Nigerian coach, after his team had played Argentina in front of 61,000 spectators; **c)-9**, said Carlos Aberto Parreira before Brazil's first game. Good job they won the title!; **d)-3**, said Jack Charlton, the Republic of Ireland manager, when complaining about the Florida heat; **e)-7** ... Bulgarian", said Hristo Stoichkov, the Bulgarian striker, after his team had sneaked through to the quarter-finals by beating Mexico in a penalty shoot-out; **f)-8**, said Arrigo Sacchi, Italy's coach, after his team had lost to the Irish republic with a full team, but beaten Norway after having a player sent off and others injured; **g)-2**, said Bertie Vogts, Germany's coach, when asked what he'd said to his team about playing in the heat; **h)-4**, said Maturana, the Colombian coach, after their defeat by USA; **i)-6**, observed TV pundit David Pleat, getting his sayings thoroughly mixed up when talking about Spain.

Kool kit

Perhaps the most startling features of the 1994 competition were the goalkeeper's jerseys. These had been growing more colourful ever since the rule that a goalkeeper could only wear a yellow, green or white jersey was abolished in 1983. Just how colourful they'd become by 1994 can be judged by what Norway's goalkeeper, Eric Thorstvedt, said when he swapped jerseys with his opposite number in the Mexican team, Jorges Campos. Said Thorstvedt, "I've been looking for new kitchen curtains for a long time"

Here are a few more wicked facts about World Cup kit:

● After the infamous match between England and Argentina in 1966, England manager Alf Ramsey was so annoyed he ran onto the pitch to stop his right-back George Cohen exchanging shirts with Argentina's Alberto Gonzales.

● Carlos Babington, a late selection for Argentina in 1974, wouldn't have given his blue-and-white striped shirt away anyhow. So delighted was he at being picked for the squad that he slept in it!

● France tried something different in 1978: swapping shirts before the match. Both they and their opponents, Hungary, had turned up for their match with their change strips – which were the same colour! France had to borrow a set of shirts from a local club.

● As for Brazil, champions in 1970, their players wore two shirts each ... well, in their minds anyway.

Their manager, Mario Zagalo, would tell the Brazilian players in team-talks that they must each wear two shirts – a defender's and an attacker's.

● Finally, for really wicked kit you can't beat the dedicated fan … and Ken Bailey, from Bournemouth, was definitely England's most dedicated fan for many years. He would turn up for games dressed as John Bull – wearing a tailcoat of hunting pink, with white breeches, a black top hat and Union Jack waistcoat. As if that wasn't enough, to complete the picture Bailey would be holding a cloth bulldog in his arms!

Host Country
FRANCE

Winners

Runners Up

No of Teams Entered **146**

Third Place

No. of Teams In Finals **32**

Fourth Place

Goals Scored

Top Scorer

*

The qualification games for the 1998 World Cup are over – and England and Scotland have both qualified for the final tournament! Yeahhh!

So, can England get through and win the trophy as they did in 1966? Can Scotland finally overcome their hoodoo and get through the first round this time? They've both been drawn in tricky groups, and neither of them have an easy game.

What a pity the Maldives didn't qualify! They're the team which, in 1997, set a World Cup record for disastrous results. Representing a scattered group of 1190 islands in the Indian Ocean, the Maldives

*Finish filling this in yourself.

competed in the Asian qualifying group. This is how they got on:

Maldives 0	Syria 12
Kyrgyztan 6	Maldives 0
Maldives 0	Kyrgyztan 3
Syria 12	Maldives 0
Maldives 0	Iran 17
Iran 9	Maldives 0

to give them a record of:

Won – 0, Drawn – 0, Lost – 6, Goals For – 0, Goals Agst – 59, Points 0

The longest game ever played?

Maldives fans may not have had much to cheer about, but that's just one of the trials a supporter has to face.

Scotland's fans had a different kind of experience in their qualifying group, as this supporter's diary reveals...

8 Oct 1996

Och! The Tartan Army are off to Estonia. Not that any of us know where it is. Still, we'll leave no Estonia unturned until we find it.

9 Oct. 1996
10 A.M.

We're here! A wee lassie at the ferry port told us the way: "Across to Finland and turn right" she said. She could have told us to pack an extra kilt or two. It's really freezing here. Estone cold, even! Scotland for Ever!!

1 PM

Good job we got to the ground nice and early. It should have been an evening kick-off but FIFA have said it's got to be played in the afternoon instead, because the Estonian floodlights aren't up to scratch. You can say that again! They look like light-bulbs on posts. Maybe they trundle them round the pitch. Useless. Everyone knows a rolling Estonian gathers no gloss!

2:50 PM

It's getting exciting now. 10 minutes to kick-off. A couple of hundred of our supporters... and just a couple of theirs! I think they know they canna beat our lads. They're looking pretty Estony faced about something....

151

152

What happened afterwards was nearly as big a shambles as the original game. The rules said that Scotland should be awarded a 3–0 win, but in the event FIFA changed their minds (and their own rules) and ordered a replay on a neutral ground which ended 0–0. The game took place on 11 February 1997, four months later – making it the longest World Cup game ever played!

> ## Wicked World Cup Quote
> Guus Hiddink, Dutch coach, after Holland beat Wales 7–1 in their qualifying group for 1998: "for five or six minutes Wales were a threat"

England beat Brazil to win World Cup trophy!

The result of the 1998 World Cup? Possibly.

But it was the result of a different type of contest which took place at Sotheby's the auctioneers on 11 July 1997. There an anonymous Englishman outbid a Brazilian insurance company to get his hands on the Jules Rimet trophy – the original World Cup, and the one Bobby Moore lifted aloft when England won it in 1966.

It cost him £245,000! And it's worth ... £100.

That's because it's not the real solid gold original but a replica, made to put on public exhibition in England to make sure the real thing didn't get stolen.

The bidders knew this (the real Jules Rimet trophy *was* stolen and melted down, remember, after Brazil won it outright in 1970) but that didn't put them off. This was the only replica in the world, and winning bidder wanted it that badly.

That's the popularity of the World Cup for you. Wicked!

Fill-it-in chart – World Cup 1998

First Round	RESULTS
Group A	
Brazil	_____
Morocco	_____
Norway	_____
Scotland	_____
Group B	
Austria	_____
Chile	_____
Cameroon	_____
Italy	_____
Group C	
Saudi Arabia	_____
Denmark	_____
France	_____
South Africa	_____
Group D	
Bulgaria	_____
Nigaria	_____
Paraguay	_____
Spain	_____

First Round	RESULTS
Group E	
Belguim	_____
Holland	_____
Mexico	_____
South Korea	_____
Group F	
Germany	_____
Iran	_____
USA	_____
Yugoslavia	_____
Group G	
Columbia	_____
England	_____
Romania	_____
Tunisia	_____
Group H	
Argentina	_____
Croatia	_____
Jamaica	_____
Japan	_____

Second Round	RESULTS

Game 1
Group A winners vs. _____
Group B runners-up _____

Game 2
Group B winners vs. _____
Group A runners-up _____

Game 3
Group C winners vs. _____
Group D runners-up _____

Game 4
Group D winners vs. _____
Group C runners-up _____

Game 5
Group E winners vs. _____
Group F runners-up _____

Game 6
Group F winners vs. _____
Group E runners-up _____

Game 7
Group G winners vs. _____
Group H runners-up _____

Game 8
Group H winners vs. _____
Group G runners-up _____

Quarter-finals

Game A
Game 1 winner vs.
Game 4 winner

Game B
Game 2 winner vs.
Game 3 winner

Game C
Game 5 winner vs.
Game 8 winer

Game D
Game 6 winner vs.
Game 7 winner

Semi-finals

Game A
Game A winner vs.
Game C winner

Game B
Game B winner vs.
Game D winner

RESULTS

_____
_____

_____
_____

_____
_____

_____
_____

_____
_____

_____
_____

Third place

Semi-final losers

Final

Semi-final winners

RESULTS

_____

_____

_____

_____